"In an age in which Iraq War and Afghan War-experienced US soldiers do not make NCO (E-4) until their second enlistment, this book reminds us that during the Vietnam War, rare but uniquely competent and mature first enlistment teenage soldiers were rewarded with combat promotions to ranks and responsibilities unattainable today without at least half a decade of experience. Doug Warden is such a soldier. This is an interesting and compelling read; a tale that is both heartening and a reminder to us all that America was lucky to have such young men serve their country during an unpopular war."

—James G. Magee, Colonel (Retired), USMC

"I have read this splendid book about the life and times of a highly decorated young sergeant who went from a boy to a man in the crucible of close combat in Vietnam...I urge you to read his account of life of the young grunts in an airmobile light infantry company and the life and death trials they faced on a daily basis."

—Charles R. Hazelip, Command Sergeant Major (Retired), US Army, Distinguished Service Cross Recipient

"This book is a very strong addition to the libraries of anyone who has served in Vietnam or knows someone who did. Anyone will enjoy reading it. A very good job!"

—Michael Christy, Lieutenant Colonel, US Army, Retired. Military Consultant to the History, Discovery and A&E Channels

"What started out as a effort to document his military service for his children has turned into what could become a best seller. Military commanders should require this book as a must read for newly minted NCO's and Second Lieutenants."
—Purple Heart Magazine, September/October, 2011

"This engaging account of war in Vietnam during the most critical period of the struggle may be read profitably on two levels. First is the story of a young man in combat, struggling to survive, just as friends fell around him. He describes the details as only one can who was there and exceptional memory remains intact, not antiseptically perhaps but not overly gory either. After all, wars have around for a long time, and not that much has changed in what happens when men engage each other with fury and determination. Yes, it's messy. On another, level, this book is the story of a young man moving from adolescence to adult hood in a world that isn't particularly friendly. That's what makes *Boy Sergeant* unique in its genre. The many episodes reveal how Warden rose to the occasion, whatever the challenge, personal and institutional. A good read, for sure."
—Charles A. Krohn, Author, Lost Battalion of Tet: The Breakout of the 2nd/12th Cavalry

"We can honestly say that your most recent book titled *Boy Sergeant* is the best 11 B (light weapons infantryman) book we have ever read, and after 40 years out of the jungle, we have read many. We want to thank you for creating such a powerful, historical, and accurate account of what our fellow combat infantrymen endured during our earlier years."
—David McAllister and Ralph Metivier, 2nd Battalion/28 Regiment, 1st Infantry Division, Vietnam

"The book is the best I've read on Vietnam since *Fields of Fire*! I am a big Jim Webb fan but *Boy Sergeant* is even better than his because it's all true."

—Tom Laney, Editor, Badger Airborne News, Badger State Chapter, 82nd Airborne Division Association

Boy Sergeant, by Doug Warden, was a book listed and reviewed on the 1st/50th Infantry Association website. I read the positive review and decided to purchase from Amazon. This is a great book to read about action on the ground in the Vietnam War. The author's honesty and easy delivery make for a fast, informative read. The book would appeal to everyone from fellow Vietnam Vets, to war historians, to younger scholars, as well as children and grandchildren of Vietnam Veterans. The book helps to explain the conditions of daily life, as well as accurate descriptions, and references of particular battles that took place.

The references to the Bong Son Plain and LZ English, and other areas of operations assigned to the 1st Cav units, were accurate and memory revitalizing. The author served with the 1st/12th Cav (Infantry) in the 1st Cav Division. I served with the 1st/50th (Mechanized) Infantry also attached to the 1st Cav Division. Doug Warden describes the Dec 15th battle at My An of the Battle of Tam Quan in which he was 100 to 200 feet from me. He describes an APC next to him being hit with an RPG round and he then moved forward to take out the NVA soldier before he could reload. My APC was one of the ones he could not help that day, as mine took an RPG round, wounding me, and taking me off the battlefield. His description of that battle filled in so many blanks in my mind from that day.

Doug Warden survived the whole year of duty in Vietnam and the rest of his book paints a true and accurate picture of a soldier that answered his country's call, and then he continued to do heroic things with his remaining military service. Better yet, he left the service and became a contributor to his country, raised a family and like any typical Vietnam Vet, kept it to himself. Thankfully, he was convinced to write down his story and publish it, so that many will benefit from his experiences and insight. This is one of the best books that I have ever read. (I became a high school English teacher after my Vietnam experience)
—C. Spotts, 1st/50th Mechanized Infantry Soldier

Although I have come to dread reading "self-published" works such as this....for a change this unedited book is very well written...with very few grammatical errors... Doug Warden tells the story of his 2 year service commitment in an excellent descriptive narrative that will definitely hold your attention! His account of his 1st Battalion, 12th Cavalry's participation with our 50th Infantry's "A" Company on December 15th in the Battle of Tam Quan helped me correct a Memorial Page error for our KIA Bernard Meinen. Thanks to Association member Mick Hawkins for recommending this book.
—Another 1st/50th Mechanized Infantry Soldier

I bought this book after reading a few other reviews and admitting I had my doubts if this author was for real. I am fully aware of the many imposters that have written books about ever being in Vietnam let alone earning valid decorations. I guess this author, Doug Warden, is the real McCoy.

This book read quickly because you won't want to put it down. His writing style is clear, flowing and smidgen with some humor and common sense. He describes his friends and others with clarity and provides commentary that you do feel comfortable who they are and how they fit into his life. The battles he's been in and ambushes are excitingly described with the right touch of graphic violence. You feel as if you're there. I rate this as an enjoyable, captivating and credible book. I enjoyed it.

—C. Lum

Well written real life action book. I was there so I can attest to the accuracy of the book. The author does a good job of describing the misery and danger of the infantry soldier.

—Bob Zawacki, "Yamaha", C Company, 1st Battalion, 12th Cavalry, 1st Cavalry

I had the honor of serving with Doug in Charlie Company for a couple of months before I rotated home. I was at An Qui with him although I was in 2nd platoon in a different part of the village when we walked into another ambush.

Doug's account is entirely accurate and an excellent read if you would like to understand what the life of a grunt was really like.

—Terry Foote C Company, 1st Battalion, 12th Cavalry, 1st Cavalry

BOY SERGEANT

DOUG WARDEN

BOY SERGEANT

A YOUNG SOLDIER'S STORY OF VIETNAM

Foreword by Colonel Robert F. Radcliffe, USA Ret.

YorkshirePublishing
www.yorkshirepublishing.com
Write Now.

ISBN: 978-1-947825-01-7
Boy Sergeant: A Young Soldier's Story of Vietnam
Copyright © 2013 by Doug Warden

Yorkshire Publishing
3207 South Norwood Avenue
Tulsa, Oklahoma 74135
www.YorkshirePublishing.com
918.394.2665

CONTENTS

FOREWORD

I am honored to have been asked to write these words as a foreword to this book written by Doug Warden. It was my great privilege to command Doug as a member of my rifle platoon in 1967, when we served together in the 1st Battalion, 12th Cavalry of the 1st Cavalry Division in the Republic of Vietnam.

Doug was an extraordinary soldier—one of those rare soldiers who instinctively make the right decisions in the most difficult of circumstances, as in close combat with a tough enemy. I'm sure he never thought of himself as a hero, but he was. He could always be counted on to move out when others would not. He could always be counted on to think clearly when others could not. He was an instinctive leader able to gain the trust of his men. He was able to balance the need to care for and protect his men while still meeting the difficult and dangerous requirements of the many missions assigned to him.

As I read his book, I was struck by his descriptions of the lessons and insights he gained, particularly in his first few days and months in combat. His observations and self-criticisms were enlightening to me, as the lessons and experiences he so eloquently describes were not apparent to me at that time. Any leader of men in combat should read and study his words, as they are a window to the soul of a man new to combat. All leaders should aspire to lead in a way that minimizes these experiences.

I have always counted Doug as a friend. I have always felt only the greatest respect for him as a combat soldier. Reading his book has only caused my love and respect for him to grow. He is the best of the best, and I am honored to have served with him.

Robert F. Radcliffe
Colonel, Infantry
United States Army, Retired

PREFACE

I never intended for the public to see this book. I wrote this account for my two adult children and my five grandchildren. Until recently, my son and daughter only knew that I had been in the army and had been to Vietnam. I had never discussed my Vietnam experience with either of them, and for that matter, anyone. My son, Rob, discovered how unique my army career was after he joined the Army ROTC in college in 1988. He took an old picture of me back to college that my wife had insisted I have made when we were stationed on Okinawa. At the time the picture was taken, I was with the 400th Army Security Agency (ASA) Special Operations Detachment, attached to the 1st Special Forces Group. My son took that picture and matched the awards and decorations I was wearing on my uniform to the Officer's Handbook he had received in Army ROTC class. He was amazed. And so, the questions from my son began ...

After I showed the manuscript of this book to a couple of people I worked with, they encouraged me to get it published. I have been reluctant to do so because I didn't want anyone thinking I was trying to make myself into a hero. I was just a scared, twenty-year-old, young man who thought he could do a better job leading soldiers than the professional non-commissioned officers (sergeants) I had observed in my short experience in the army. Most of our sergeants treated their men like little kids. They berated them and almost never gave them any words of encouragement. They also sent them to do jobs like fill sand bags, pull guard duty on the perimeter or on a listening post (LP), burn human excrement, and walk point. I thought that I wasn't any better than anyone else, so I shared the work with the men assigned to me. I never asked anyone to do something that I hadn't done myself. I got my own C rations, made my own poncho tent, and I took turns walking point and pulling guard duty with the guys in my squad. I also didn't send my men into combat; I was out front leading them. I learned these qualities from some of the great officers that we had in our company. So, after some final encouragement from my son, Rob, here is my story of Vietnam.

This is the story of my year in Vietnam with an infantry company in combat. For the better part of that year, I was part of a group of men who ran toward the sound of gunfire, rather than away from it. Firemen and law enforcement officers will know what I mean. All of us who were infantrymen with the 1st Cavalry Division are proud of the fact we never ran and never retreated in combat.

This time in my life is special to me and to others who served in my unit, because for most of us, it was the high point of our lives. Almost every one of our decisions and actions had life or death consequences. Walking point at a fast pace could be life threatening. Sending one of your men down a tunnel with a pistol and a flashlight put his life in jeopardy. Identifying the unit in a mistaken place on the map had major consequences. A small mistake that resulted in a casualty could have your men doubt your judgment for the rest of your tour and result in the men refusing to follow your guidance. Every time we had people firing bullets at us, there were a number of men who looked at me for leadership. I had to make hard, fast decisions on the fly. I can't say I never made a mistake, but I never hesitated to do something, even if it was wrong. Most of the time, doing nothing was the wrong choice.

As a draftee, I went to Vietnam as a private first class (E-3) and became one of the youngest staff sergeants (E-6) in the Army. I was barely twenty years old and responsible for the feeding, clothing, health, and general wellbeing of a squad or platoon of men in combat—most of whom were older than I was. I was responsible for keeping them alive while accomplishing the missions we were sent on every day. Due to luck more than anything, no one assigned to me lost his life. Several occasions demanded that I become the platoon sergeant or the platoon leader while our unit was in contact with the enemy. That meant I called in artillery, positioned the men, coordinated with the company commander, and led assaults on enemy positions. All other life experiences pale in comparison to that kind of responsibility.

Most of the other staff sergeants in our infantry company had been in the army for at least five to fifteen years. I had been in the Army for less than eighteen months. Most of my peers resented me. They referred to me as "Boy Sergeant," though never to my face. The guys in my platoon called me "Audie Murphy, Jr."—and it embarrassed me to no end when I heard them call me that.

While in Vietnam, I served with the 3rd platoon of Charlie Company, 1st Battalion (Airborne), 12th Cavalry,

1st Air Cavalry Division. Charlie Company was a legend in Vietnam. The company was awarded the Presidential Unit Citation three times and the Valorous Unit Award three times while in Vietnam. Two of the Presidential Unit Citations and two of the Valorous Unit Awards were given at the company level (others were awarded at the division level). I was with Charlie Company when it was awarded the Valorous Unit Award at the company level for actions on May 31–June 1, 1967, at the Battle of An Qui.

While with Charlie Company, I was shot twice (both flesh wounds) and sustained shrapnel wounds when I was blown several feet in the air by a grenade that went off between my legs. In July 1967, a CH-54 "Flying Crane" transporting a 155 mm howitzer to LZ (landing zone) Arbuckle in the Central Highlands crashed and burned on top of my foxhole. I barely escaped in time. I came close to stepping on two booby traps; one, an unexploded 155 mm round, that certainly would have killed Lt. Bob Radcliffe, my platoon leader, and me. Toward the end of my tour, as I was flying away from the field for the last time going from Quang Tri to An Khe, the C-130 carrying my former commanding officer, Capt. Pete Bentson, another sergeant and me, emergency crash-landed at the Da Nang Air Base when the hydraulics were damaged by small arms fire.

I never meant for my army career to go as it did. I never meant to volunteer for a tour of duty in Vietnam. When I was eighteen, my goal in life was to be a schoolteacher and basketball coach. They made two hundred dollars a week. To make that kind of money required a college degree. I wanted to go in, serve my two years, and get out so I could get back to college. But I grew up in the army. It changed me from a carefree, immature, nineteen-year-old kid to a responsible adult by the time I got out six years later. The army was good to me in many ways, and I have only good things to say about my experiences. Both of my children were born in army hospitals. My son was born at Ft. Devens, MA, in 1970, and my daughter at Camp Kue, Okinawa, Japan in 1971. The army retired me with disability on March 1, 1973. While serving with the 1st Special Forces Group on Okinawa, I was injured when the anchor line cable failed during a practice jump in jumpmaster school from a thirty-four-foot parachute tower. That I survived this fall is miraculous, but it is even more miraculous that I survived up to that time. Because of my injuries, I was able to attend college on the GI bill as a disabled veteran. I graduated in 1980 with a BA in management from Webster College in St. Louis, MO and eventually did some graduate work toward an MBA.

If I were to hear some man in his mid-sixties telling my story, I would immediately think he was the biggest liar in the country and a phony to boot. My story is hard to believe. Even now, as I think about that time, I find it difficult to believe, but it is true. My good friend, Bob Radcliffe, has been kind enough to write a foreword to this story. He can vouch for the truthfulness of this story, as can others. He and I were hardly ever over a couple of steps apart for my first four months in country. David Wilkowski, Earl Osborne, Cliff Metz, Tom "Doc" Jensen, Michael "Doc" Leroy, Buster Morgan, Alvin Nibbelink, Rich Valles, Billy Cabaniss, Joe "Doc" O'Keefe, and Charles Fletcher were also with me over the course of a year. As far as I know, they are all still alive as I write this.

The reason I cite all these people is because in the book *Stolen Valor*, B.G. Burkett of Dallas, Texas, describes a number of veterans and non-veterans who have lied about serving in Vietnam, the units they were with and the awards and decorations they received. Burkett writes about meeting a group of so-called veterans in Texas who dressed in camouflage fatigues, wore their hair long, and claimed to be Navy SEALs, Green Berets, and Force Recon Marines. They all turned out to be liars, or as Burkett calls them, "wannabes." Some had never been in the military, and most had never been to Vietnam—and if they had been, not in combat. In light of that, I am including as much documented proof as possible at the end of this narrative.

By the way, I would recommend Burkett's book. It clears up a number of mistaken stigmas about Vietnam vets. The book concludes what I have felt for a number of years. That is, that most Vietnam veterans came back home and resumed normal lives. These Vietnam veterans raised families, worked well at their jobs, were involved in their communities, and became role models. I think the main reason they have become productive members of society is because they have a certain appreciation for life.

Nowadays, I don't talk much about Vietnam unless I get around other combat veterans. And I certainly don't tell about the bad times I experienced to anyone. Most people, even my close friends, do not know about the events that happened to me while I was in Vietnam from May 14, 1967, to May 1, 1968. This narrative is my way of revealing the whole story. This book is compiled from my memories. Those memories are sometimes fuzzy, since almost forty-three years have passed, but most of my memories are as clear as if they happened last year. If there are any factual errors in my telling, the mistakes are my own, and I take sole responsibility for them.

One of things I promised myself when I started this book was to tell the truth. What that means is you are going to read about the good, the bad, and the ugly regarding combat, my friends, my enemies, and me. I recently saw someone wearing a tee shirt with the message, "The older I get, the better I was." I have tried to make sure I didn't make the stories here anymore than they really were.

Part of the "ugly" I have not included, however, is the bad language I heard, nor have I written about the prostitution and sex that surrounded us both during operations and when we came in from the field. You can learn about those things from other books and narratives.

I told my mom and dad very little about my year in Vietnam when I returned home. I should have, but I felt my mom would not have been proud of some of the things I did during my tour of duty. I never even told my folks I jumped out of airplanes. I didn't want them to worry. I brought my mom a lot of heartache before I turned twenty-one years old, and I didn't want to bring her more by revealing some of the things that are in this book.

She prayed every day for me while I was in Vietnam. I feel that I wouldn't have made it out alive if not for her support and faith. She received three telegrams during that year to inform her and Dad that I was wounded in action. I know each of those notices tore at her heart. Mom died June 10, 1997, while I was holding her hand. I lost a very dear friend. My dad accidentally set fire to his house on February 26, 2005, and died of smoke inhalation. I miss both of them a lot.

As I thought about attending my first 1st Cav and 12th Cav reunions in 2005, I was concerned I would run into someone I hadn't gotten along with or someone I offended by the decisions I made while I was a leader in our platoon. Nobody can please everybody. I was stupid, insensitive, conceited, wise, decisive, and lucky, all at the same time. The memories bring embarrassment, doubt, sadness, happiness, dread, horror, and pride.

At least I did something, and I honestly can say I did the best I could. I am reassured by some comments I've heard. Jerry Richards, who was in my squad, told me, "When I became a squad leader, I tried to do things just like you did them." I also heard from Alan Van Dan, who wrote for the 12th Cav newsletter, after he visited Dave Carmody, my last platoon leader in Charlie Company. I had been so insolent to Lt. Carmody on any number of occasions. When I would hear him say to the troops something I considered stupid, I would call him aside and bluntly say things like, "Sir, that's the stupidest thing I've ever heard an officer say!" or, "Sir, you just don't understand the way things are!" I expected Alan to tell me that Lt. Carmody never wanted to see or hear from me. Instead, Carmody told Alan that my instruction and counsel to him was the main reason he remained alive during his service in Vietnam.

Tears came into my eyes on both of these occasions. It told me I had nothing to fear from seeing anyone I served with in Vietnam.

In March 2002, while traveling on business in Washington, DC, my wife called to tell me that my old friend, David Wilkowski from my squad, had called me. I was ecstatic. I had heard from David only one time after he left the field in early January 1968, and that was when he sent me two pints of bourbon while I was still in Vietnam. There was no note and there didn't need to be. He was making good on a promise to send some bourbon to me and Phillip Hayes, who was also in my squad.

When I arrived home the next day, I called him. He had found a note I posted on an Internet message service for locating Vietnam buddies. He said he had told his wife and family that I was a really smart guy and he expected me to be a senator or university professor. I had always thought Wilkowski was smart until I heard him state this impression of me! We talked about old times and all the guys we knew, and at the end of our conversation, I told him I loved him like a brother. He replied, "Doug, you are my brother." Even though it wasn't the manly thing to do, when I hung up, I cried. To have one of the bravest and best guys I have ever known tell me I was his brother after over thirty-five years, stirred emotions in me I hadn't felt in years.

I met some of the best guys in the world while in Vietnam. I also served with some guys whom I wouldn't walk across the street to see again. War brings out the best and worst of people. War brought out the best of draftees Sgt. Dennis Rasmussen, Sgt. Billy Cabaniss, Sgt. Rick Boeshart (KIA December 15, 1967), Spec. 4th Class Tom Cusick (deceased), Sgt. Phillip Hayes (deceased), Sgt. Cliff Metz, Sgt. Charles Fletcher, Sgt. Buster Morgan, Sgt. Rich Valles, Sgt. David Wilkowski, Spec. 5th Class Tom "Doc" Jensen, Spec. 5th Class Joe "Doc" O'Keefe, Spec. 5th Class Michael "Doc" Leroy, and Sgt. Earl Osborne.

It also brought out the best in 1st Lt. Bob Radcliffe, West Point class of 1965 (now a retired full colonel) and Capt. Pete Bentson, West Point class of 1963 (later a major, KIA in Vietnam in 1972).

It is to these men named above, the men who were killed while serving with Charlie Company, and my children, Rob Warden and April Warden Humphrey, who encouraged me to write this story, that I dedicate this book.

Doug Warden, 2010

PART I:
BEFORE VIETNAM

OKLAHOMA CHILDHOOD

I was born in the town of Prague, OK, in 1947. My dad paid twenty-five dollars to Dr. John Rollins for the delivery. My dad was Robert C. "Short" Warden, a farmer just like his father and every one of our Warden ancestors since they came to America around 1770.

We lived on eighty acres, two and a half miles south of Prague. Dad usually had two jobs because farming didn't pay a lot. So he worked as a roughneck, roustabout, custodian, or plumber and then came home and got on his 1946 Ford tractor to plow or cultivate, or he would go out to the barn to repair some equipment. He could never afford new farm equipment or home appliances. When they needed repair, he ordered parts or made them. We never had much in the way of material goods, but Dad kept everything in good working order. I've always thought my dad would have made a great mechanical engineer given the opportunity for an education. Dad was not even sure he finished the seventh grade. His dad needed him to help work their farm. He was the oldest of seven children, so he went to work full time with Grandpa Warden on their rented farm when he was thirteen years old.

In 1939, he got a job with the Civilian Conservation Corps and worked around Yuma, AZ, on the trails leading down into the Grand Canyon. He thought Grandpa and Grandma Warden would have an easier time feeding six rather than seven kids, and he could make some money and get free room and board. He joined the US Army Air Corps early in 1941 and was already on active duty when Pearl Harbor was bombed in December 1941. He was a mess sergeant for the US Army Air Corps in St. Louis, MO, traveling in troop trains and cooking for the soldiers being shipped out to the east and west coasts. He shipped out to Panama and served there until the war was over. After WWII, he and Mom bought the family farm in January 1948, where he resided until he died in 2005. Dad met Mom just after he returned home from the CCC camps in 1940. She was a sophomore in high school in Paden, Oklahoma. Grandma Warden would save some money from selling eggs in town and give Dad one dollar to spend on dates with Mom. Dad would borrow his folk's old Model A Ford and have enough to put in some gas, pay for a movie and have enough left over for popcorn and gum. Grandpa Suggs would not consent to Mom marrying Dad, so they waited until she turned eighteen on the 29th of October in 1942 and they married two days later. My mom, Katherene Suggs Warden, was valedictorian of her high school class and voted best actress by her classmates for her portrayals of elderly women in the junior and senior plays. She wanted to go to college when she graduated from high school in 1942, but that was impossible because her father could not afford to send any of his children to college. She went to work as a legal secretary when I was in the seventh grade and worked in the legal profession for over twenty-five years.

We lived in a small frame house that had no insulation or electricity until I was six years old and no plumbing until I was nine. I slept in a small bedroom in the back of the house. When winter came, we would close off the bedrooms and heat only the front room and kitchen. Bedtime meant I would make a beeline to my bedroom and get under the sheets and four or five quilts. I walked half a mile north to catch the school bus at 7:30 a.m., and then I walked home in the afternoon. I've always joked that I had to walk uphill both ways, and it's true. I would walk uphill a quarter mile to the crest of the hill and then a quarter mile downhill to the mile section line and the intersection of the dirt roads where I boarded the bus.

I was an only child until I was five years old. That's when my sister, Jenny, was born. Before Jenny came along, I was Mom's student and experiment, since Dad's jobs took him away from home for twelve-hour days and after that he farmed. Mom read to me a lot. I could read and write when I began the first grade in the fall of 1953. My teacher, Mrs. Bertha Cash, had also taught my dad when he was in school. She promoted me to the second grade after just nine weeks of school. This made me the youngest student in my class for the rest of my school career.

I attended a little country school in Centerview, three miles south of Prague. I also attended several different schools as we moved around with Dad when he worked as a roughneck in the oilfields. We lived in a little sixteen-foot trailer when away from the farm. My bed was one of the seats for the dining table. I thought it was so neat to wake up, sit up, and be at the breakfast table in the morning.

We lived in Snyder, Texas, and three places in Oklahoma—Beaver, Altus, and Shawnee—while Dad worked in the oilfields.

After moving back to the farm when I was in the seventh grade, I graduated from the eighth grade with seven other students; five of us were white kids and three were Native American kids that were all related to Jim Thorpe, the legendary Native American athlete. He was born about three miles from our farm home. Centerview eventually lost its high school in 1961, because there were less than forty students in attendance in the ninth through the twelfth grades. I graduated from Prague High School with a "big" class of thirty-six in May 1964. I had been sixteen for most of my senior year; I turned seventeen in April and graduated in May.

As a youngster, I worked as a shoeshine boy, pumped gas, and hauled hay to get spending money to pay for my own clothes. I wasn't much help to my dad on the farm. I had asthma or hay fever. I had to wear a wet rag around my face when I worked around wheat, hay or corn. I'm also ashamed to admit I just didn't want to do farm work. I wasn't interested in it, and I saw no future to it. My work ethic was less than satisfactory. I did do chores around the farm, though, because Dad usually was working either in the evening or morning. So, I would feed hay to our cows, slop fifty or so hogs, and milk a cow.

I was a good kid and a straight A student until the seventh grade. That's when I began to break the rules at school and home. I started smoking and using bad language. I don't know why I became rebellious. Maybe it was because I was a year younger than my classmates and had to prove I was just as big and tough as they were. Maybe I was rebelling against my strict, church-going upbringing. It was probably because my friends did the same things. I desperately wanted to be accepted by them.

I started committing petty crimes in high school. I didn't murder anybody or rob liquor stores, but I stole things in out-of-town clothing stores, drank beer and whiskey before my sixteenth birthday, and wrote several hot checks to keep up with the spending of my buddies. I shudder to think of what I might have become had circumstances not been different. Mom and Dad were unaware of my illegal behavior, but they observed enough from my bad attitude and sullen looks to try to correct me. I just never listened. I can still remember Dad telling me, "You'll never amount to a hill of beans!" Had I kept exhibiting the same behavior much longer, he would have been right.

My academic career was less than splendid in high school. I did just enough to get by. It was something I would regret later in life when I went back to college with a different attitude. I played every sport at Prague High. I was really too skinny for football, but I played my senior year. I had several twenty-point games in basketball, and I was the catcher for the baseball team.

I wasn't with the "in" crowd, if there was such a group at my school. I tried hard to be a good friend to the friends I had, but I wasn't popular. My prospects for college were dim because my mom and dad couldn't afford to help, and I didn't have a scholarship. I completed one semester of college at Eastern Oklahoma A&M in Southeastern Oklahoma. My part-time job at the junior college was in the student union, so I became a good pool and snooker player. I tried out for the basketball team but quit after I made the traveling squad. I had a real "loser" attitude.

By the end of the semester, I was tired of being broke and tired of being hungry all the time. The cafeteria didn't feed me enough, and I didn't have enough money to buy food off campus. I was mad at everybody and everything. So, I quit. I know that disappointed my mom. She wanted me to have a college education. When I turned eighteen in April 1965, I registered at my local draft board and was classified 1-A.

GERMANY

Military service was always a given for me. My dad served with the US Army Air Corps in World War II as an enlisted man and became a staff sergeant. His brother, Raymond, was in combat in Korea and retired as a sergeant first class from the army. My mother's brother, Bob Suggs, served with the artillery in Germany. Samuel Warden, my fourth great grandfather and earliest ancestor in America who lived near Charlotte, N.C., was a Scotch-Irish immigrant who served for three years with the Army of North Carolina in the Revolutionary War. His name is among those engraved in the side of the county courthouse in Anniston, AL, as a tribute to Revolutionary War veterans. A maternal fourth great grandfather, Jacob Prevett, served with the same army from Iredell County, N.C. Samuel Warden's four sons served in the War of 1812. Most of their sons, one of whom was my great-great grandfather, served on both sides in the Civil War.

There was never any question I would go into the service. When your country called, you went. The only unknown was, when? Like most boys, I played war as a youngster. I had seen John Wayne movies, and I always wanted to be the hero who was honest, fair, and got the girl. A couple of my second-grade friends and I were play-ing one day when one of my friends acted as if he were shot.

As he lay on the ground pretending to die, he told me, "Tell my mom and dad that I love them!" I cried because it moved me so.

My draft notice arrived in April 1966, just after my nineteenth birthday. I was working at Tinker Air Force Base in Oklahoma City tearing down J-57 jet engine man-ifolds. I lived in a nice, furnished apartment and drove a baby blue, 1962 Chevrolet Impala Super Sport with leather bucket seats and a 327 cubic inch V-8 engine. I celebrated my nineteenth birthday in Prague at the L&O Bar. I had used my fake ID so much that they all thought I was twenty-one. Sometime that night a local oilfield worker accused me of offending his friend and invited me outside to teach me a lesson. I paused to drink the rest of my beer, and he hit me in the back of the head. The fight started at the front of the bar and ended about one hundred feet back from the bar. He never hit me again after the first punch. I blackened both his eyes and bloodied his nose before the fight was stopped.

I have often wondered if someone turned my name in so I would be drafted early. I wouldn't blame them if they did. I had no direction in my life, no goals or objectives, no girlfriend, and was headed for trouble. I entered the army on June 28, 1966, as a private E-1. Pay was seventy-eight dollars per month then.

All of the guys heading for the army from Pottawatomie County, OK, were bused to the induction station in Oklahoma City and then flown from Oklahoma City to Dallas Love Field and on to Fort Polk, LA, to the reception station. It was my first time on an airplane. We flew on a

Frontier Airlines jet from Oklahoma City to Dallas Love Field. From there, we flew on an old DC3 to Fort Polk. There we were issued uniforms, got our haircuts, drew partial pay of twenty dollars and spent thirteen days pulling details around post. After going through the clothing line, I was issued more clothes and footwear than I had ever owned in my life. The Army recorded my blood type at that time as Type A. When I re-enlisted after my Vietnam service, they recorded it as type O+. I argued with them, but they retested and got the same results. If I had ever needed a blood transfusion in Vietnam, it would have killed me.

I didn't know it at the time, but we were waiting at the Fort Polk reception station for Fort Bragg, NC, to open up for basic training for the first time since the end of WWII. We were flown to Pope Air Force Base and transported to Fort Bragg to begin our training. The US Army's Special Forces soldiers conducted most of our basic training because we were short of drill instructors. After Fort Bragg, I was assigned to the Advanced Infantry School at Fort Ord in California. I received my MOS (military occupational specialty) of 11B, which signifies light weapons infantry.

I saw guys trying anything to get out the army, both in basic training and advanced infantry training. Some tried to elevate their blood sugar, some tried drinking large amounts of coffee and still others tried to fail the urine tests. The only ploy that I saw work was at Fort Ord. A soldier in my training company went to the PX (Post Exchange) and bought a jar of crunchy peanut butter. In our latrines we had the old commodes that had pull strings. That meant they didn't have any standing water in the commode. This guy put the jar of peanut butter in the commode and had one of his buddies run to get the sergeant on duty, the CQ (charge of quarters). When the sergeant came into the latrine, the soldier put his hand into the commode and pulled out a wad of peanut butter and ate it. The sergeant thought he was eating his own feces and ran out of the barracks gagging. The next morning, the guy was gone. He was out of the army. They didn't want anything to do with him. We couldn't get anyone to even talk about what had happened.

After volunteering to be a paratrooper when I was at Fort Ord, I then spent the next few months in Germany with an infantry unit, where I was just miserable. We stood guard with no ammunition and simulated foxholes in the frozen ground by drawing a circle around ourselves in the snow. One particular day, I was up most of the night on guard duty and was immediately put in the armory cleaning weapons the rest of the next day. Even though I was really trying to be a good trooper, I stayed in constant trouble with my recon platoon sergeant, to the point that he slapped me several times because I made him look bad to the "Old Man."

We had big-time racial problems in Germany. Someone stole all of my fatigue jackets out of my locker. I caught the guy, who happened to be black, in the chow hall wearing my fatigue blouse. I knew it was mine and accosted him. He denied it was mine, but I knew if I could get it off him, my laundry mark would be inside. I decked him right there in the mess hall and started to take his shirt off. About four or five black soldiers jumped me to defend him. They landed several punches on me, until a few of the sergeants broke it up. That afternoon I was in front of the company commander. He did not give me any non-judicial punishment, but my platoon sergeant put me on extra detail for the next month.

Most infantrymen would have loved to serve their tour in Germany and avoid Vietnam, but I was miserable. I finally had enough one day. I went down to the orderly room with my buddy, Wayne Lynch of El Sobrante, CA, and we both submitted Form 1049 to request service in Vietnam.

Wayne was sore because our captain had relieved him of his clerk's job and had put him in my squad in an infantry slot. But he really didn't have much to worry about. Because he had a clerk's MOS, he would get a clerk's job in Vietnam. On the other hand, I knew where I was going as a light weapons infantryman. I was 11 Bravo, or as we called it in Vietnam, "11 Bush." In Germany we were supposed to be soldiers, but were playing at war. I saw no sense to it. I hated it, and I wanted out at any cost. I also think deep down inside I wanted to see if I could prove myself in the real thing.

I arrived home in March 1967, for a thirty-day leave. I was out every night, drinking and carousing, until my time came to leave. I called some officer in California to ask for an extension to get married. I had no intention of getting married and had no prospects, but I knew I would someday, so I thought I really wasn't lying. I got a fifteen-day extension. The powers that be never checked to see if I really did get married.

When my time finally came to leave for California, I arranged for one of my friends, Don Heinzig, to pick me up and take me to Oklahoma City in his Corvette. Before he arrived at the farm, I went in to tell Mom good-bye. Mama collapsed on the floor of her bedroom, crying uncontrollably. With tears in my eyes, I went into Jenny's bedroom to tell her good-bye, and she retreated to the closet and closed the door. With more tears in my eyes, I began to walk with Dad out to the barn and talk with him. We got about halfway to the barn where the cows were kept, when Dad dropped his milk bucket and fell to the ground.

He cried, "I just can't stand you leaving like this. We might never see you again!" I was so choked up with emotion when Don came to pick me up, I couldn't talk for several minutes.

As was usual for me, I had never thought what effect my actions had on other people. Up until that moment, I had never thought anybody cared about me. My opinion of myself was so low that I never had a thought my mom, dad, and sister loved me very much. I felt pretty rotten, but there was no turning back now. I had been ordered to report to Oakland Army Terminal in California for transportation to the Republic of Vietnam.

Don dropped me off at Tinker Air Force Base before eight o'clock in the morning. By noon, I was on a military aircraft to California. An engine on the plane caught fire over the Oklahoma Panhandle, and we had to return to Tinker. The next plane they put me on was a general's jet. I was the only enlisted man on the aircraft. When I arrived at Travis Air Force Base in California, I called Norman Opela—a guy I had gone to high school with who was at Two-Rock Ranch, an army security agency installation near Petaluma, CA. I stayed with him a couple of days before I had to report. He took me out one night to a go-go nightclub in Santa Rosa where the girls danced topless with pasties on their breasts. It was a remarkable sight for a farm boy from Oklahoma.

The reality of what I had done and where I was going began to hit me when I reported to Oakland Army

Terminal. There I met a guy named Larry Ashley from somewhere in Texas. He had just married his high school sweetheart, and I could tell he loved his wife very much. He and I would stay together for the trip to Vietnam and join the same infantry unit in Vietnam. He would leave the field in June 1967, after a booby trap with a 155 mm artillery shell went off near him.

After a couple of days of evading KP (kitchen police, which was working in the mess hall) and work details at Oakland, they bused us to Travis Air Force Base for the trip to Vietnam. They filled up a leased jetliner with guys from all branches of the armed services. I remember we stopped a couple of times to refuel, but I don't know where. I do remember we stopped in the Philippines to spend the night, so the flight crew could sleep. Our next stop was Vietnam.

PART II:
IN COUNTRY

CHARLIE COMPANY

We touched down on the runway at Pleiku Air Base on May 14, 1967. When I stepped out on the ramp to the airplane, I felt a heat that almost took my breath away. The summer before my one semester of college, I worked at a roofing manufacturing plant in Oklahoma City unloading 110-pound sacks of slate from railroad cars. Until I arrived in Vietnam, I thought I had experienced the most heat ever in those railroad cars. I was wrong.

I looked around to see if they had rifles ready for us. All I saw was an airman standing behind a machine gun, patrolling in a jeep with another airman driving. I didn't know it then, but we were in a very safe area, as safe as any place in Vietnam. As the duty sergeant assigned us to our bunks, he remarked, "This is the birthplace of Ho Chi Minh, and the Viet Cong would love to capture it." Later I learned nobody knew much about Ho, least of all where he was born. The sergeant could have been serious, but was probably trying to scare a bunch of new troops. I remember we spent the night there, and each man had to spend time pulling guard duty in the bunkers surrounding the sleeping quarters. It was so hot that I thought I would never get to sleep.

The next day, I learned I was assigned to the 1st Air Cavalry Division headquartered at An Khe in the Central Highlands of Vietnam. My original orders were for me to join the long-range reconnaissance company for the 1st Cav. A large group of us was guided in the stifling heat to the floor of a C-130 Air Force propeller-driven airplane for the trip to Camp Radcliffe near An Khe. I worried the plane was overloaded because they put about a hundred and fifty of us on the plane. The trip to the An Khe airstrip took about forty-five minutes. We were trucked to the 15th Administration Company where our company assignments were made. I was assigned to Company C (Charlie Company), 1st Battalion (Airborne), 12th Cavalry. My company was part of the 1st Brigade, an all-airborne brigade now designated "leg." That is, some non-airborne personnel were being integrated with the paratroopers of the 1st Brigade.

The 1st Air Cavalry Division was the first full division to be sent to Vietnam in August 1965. The 173rd Airborne Brigade and a brigade of the 101st Airborne Division, as well as several thousand Marines, had been deployed before the 1st Air Cavalry.

Prior to 1967, I didn't know much about the 1st Cav. The Cav had been assembled from various units at Fort Benning, Ga., in 1963 and 1964 as the 11th Air Assault (Test) to develop and test the new airmobile concepts brought about by the Army's Howse Board. The whole division had already received the Presidential Unit Citation for their action in the Ia Drang Valley in October and November 1965.

The division had three brigades. The 1st Brigade had been all airborne (parachutist qualified) and was made up of the 1st and 2nd Battalions, 8th Cavalry, and the 1st Battalion, 12th Cavalry. The 2nd Brigade was airmobile and made up of the 1st and 2nd Battalions, 5th Cavalry, and the 2nd Battalion, 12th Cavalry. The 3rd Brigade was the 1st, 2nd, and 5th Battalions of the 7th Cavalry. An additional scout and recon unit was the 1st/9th Battalion of the 1st Cavalry Division. Other units also with the Cav were the 1st Battalion, 50th Infantry (Mechanized), the 15th Administration Company (which had over a thousand men assigned to it), the 227th, 228th and 229th Aviation Companies and H Company (Airborne), 75th Rangers (formerly E Company (Airborne), 52nd Infantry). There were also artillery battalions attached to each brigade.

Charlie Company, 1st Battalion (Airborne), 12th Cavalry, was part of the 1st Brigade and had been in many famous battles. In May 1966, the company lost fourteen of nineteen men from the mortar platoon at the battle of LZ Hereford. Later that year, Charlie Company earned a Presidential Unit Citation as the assault force at Hoa Hoi. On December 17, 1966, they were at the Battle of 506 Valley and lost seven killed and dozens wounded. And then in late December 1966, the company lost fourteen infantrymen and over twenty artillerymen when LZ Bird was overrun in the Central Highlands. Larry Register, a friend of mine in the 1st platoon who was at LZ Bird, saved himself by playing dead while an NVA (North Vietnamese Army) soldier sat on him in the darkness and smoked a cigarette. Charlie Company was awarded another Presidential Unit Citation for LZ Bird.

After getting our assignments at the 15th Administration Company, I was trucked with a few others, including Larry

Ashley, my newly married friend from Texas, Charles Church, a college graduate from North Carolina, Charley Waskey, an Aluetian Indian from Alaska, and Perry Benally, a Navajo Indian from New Mexico, to the rear area of Charlie Company. We were issued our combat gear, which included an M-16 rifle, magazines, web gear, back pack, ammo pouches, steel helmet, jungle fatigues, air mattress, mosquito net, waterproof bag, sleeping bag, socks, two pair of jungle boots, and a minimum amount of ammo.

The next day we were back to the 15th Admin Company for a three-day crash course in how the Cav operated. Our instructors told us to forget everything we had been taught in infantry school because this was a "different" war.

The cadre, all combat veterans, explained, "There are no front lines here. You are about to meet an enemy who does not play by the rules of engagement. They will harass you with booby traps and occasional sniper fire. You may never see them until they outnumber you and are assured of victory."

It was here I did something that terrified me even more than jumping out of airplanes—rappelling. The Cav used rappelling down a rope as a means of infiltrating the jungle from helicopters when they cannot land. I don't know how high the towers were, but the instructor who showed me how to hook my D ring into the rope had to steady my trembling hands. The D ring was secured to us in a Swiss seat harness, a ten-foot piece of rope tied around the waist and under the crotch. We had to go down a side of the tower where boards simulated a sheer cliff.

We zeroed our weapons, listened to a lot of briefings, and on the second day of training, were ready to go outside the wire for more instruction. Outside the "green line" or the barbwire perimeter at An Khe, the terrain was marked by sparse vegetation. There were some scrub trees and knee-high grass. We watched an ARA (aerial rocket artillery) demonstration performed by a Huey gunship and crew. It was impressive. The pilot made a couple of runs and fired some rockets. Then one gunship dumped his entire ordinance—all forty-eight of its 2.75-inch rockets—at once on a target in front of us. It was even more impressive.

We attended more classes. The instructors cautioned us to load eighteen rounds in our twenty-round magazines because the M-16 rifles we had were prone to jam. On the evening of our second day of training, we spent our first night outside the wire with everybody in our class, which included new cooks, truck drivers, clerks, artillerymen, infantrymen and our instructors. We all ate our C rations, blew up our air mattresses, and got into sleeping bags. It was the last time I slept in a sleeping bag for the next ten months. It was an uneventful night. We didn't know then, but there was a company of veteran infantry nearby watching over us. We had made it through our first "dangerous" night in country. It was the beginning of many, many more nights for me outside the wire.

WAR AND BEAUTY

I don't remember much about the next couple of nights after I returned to Charlie Company's rear area. Because I believed I was going to die, I had sworn to myself and to God I would not drink or swear ever again. That promise was kept for about two hours. It was that night at the bar that I met Staff Sgt. Delbert O. Jennings. He introduced himself as my new squad leader. I drank several screwdrivers with him, and he seemed like a nice guy. He was taking all the new guys including me out to the field the next day. I heard from the other guys he wasn't supposed to go back out to the field because he had been recommended for the Medal of Honor for the LZ Bird battle.

I also met our company clerk, though I don't remember his name. He had arrived on LZ Bird on Christmas Day 1966, only to be overrun and wounded after spending two nights in the field. After he returned to the rear area, they needed a clerk typist and he got the job. All my early bravado from Germany had already vanished, and I wished I were he, so I could be in the rear and go home alive. I do recall his personality was belligerent. He was arrogant and everything out of his mouth was condescending to the new guys.

I also met someone who would become one of my life-long friends. He was our executive officer (XO) and was about to go out in the next few days and continue his field time as a platoon leader with us. His name was Robert F. Radcliffe. A native of Marblehead, MA, he was a first lieutenant, West Point class of 1965, graduated way down in his class and proud of it, a senior parachutist who had served with the 82nd Airborne, and a Ranger school graduate. He was to have the most profound effect on my life.

I met two black guys who just stayed in the bunkhouse and drank beer. They were Robert O. Smith ("Smitty") and David Black—two buck sergeants slated to go home soon. They couldn't say anything to any of us new guys without reminding us how "short" they were. Being a short-timer meant the person didn't have many days to go before he went back to the "world." Someone told me that Smitty was the most decorated soldier of the battalion. If I remember correctly, he had been awarded two Bronze Stars, two Purple Hearts, and the Soldier's Medal, the highest award for life saving. They both sat around and told us war story after war story. Black was with Headquarters Company and was a lineman with a Signal Corp MOS. That didn't keep him from being "volunteered" to pull LRP (long-range patrol) duty. If half the stories they told us were true, they were both good men.

Charles Church, Larry Ashley, Perry Benally, Charlie Waskey and I had a lot of time to sit around and speculate on what it was going to be like for us in the field with the company. Charles, Larry and I did most of the talking, since Perry and Charlie were for the most part very quiet. Perry Benally was from New Mexico and had lived on and off a Navajo reservation since childhood. English was a second language to Perry. He spoke fluent Navajo. Charlie Waskey had a similar background and had lived in an Aleutian village all his life. Charlie was solidly built, had slanted eyes and was about 5 foot 8 inches tall. We all agreed that he better wear his green fatigues at all times, lest he be mistaken for the enemy. Perry Benally was slightly built and was about 5 foot 6 inches tall. Neither man would have impressed anyone as a soldier. I never heard either man utter over twenty words in the three days of training that we had gone through. Church and Ashley hit it off almost immediately. They had great rapport among themselves as we sat around and talked. Mostly we talked about what we were going to do when we got away from Vietnam and returned stateside.

The night before we were to go out to the field, Charles Church was bitten by a rat while he was sleeping. He went to the medical aid station and was ordered confined to quarters in order to take a series of rabies shots in his abdomen. While he was in the rear on profile, someone discovered he had a college degree and could type, so he became the company clerk. I was glad to know that Charles was replacing the jerk that had the job.

The next day, we were driven to the "Golf Course," the heliport for the Cav. If you can imagine a landing strip long enough for C-130 airplanes to take off and land, surrounded by landing pads for over for hundred helicopters, then you can begin to get a sense of how big this place was. It had been cut with axes and machetes by the advance party of the Cav in 1965, when a general ordered the grass left to keep down the dust and debris that was normally strewn by the helicopters taking off and landing. He wanted a heliport smooth enough to be a golf course (hence the name). We boarded a Huey and headed for Bong Son, over on the coast on Highway 1, at the mouth of the Bong Son River. We arrived at forward headquarters for the 1st Brigade about forty minutes later.

Our brigade commander at that time was Col. Donald Rattan. The commander of the 1st Battalion, 12th Cav was Lt. Col. Loyd Riddlehoover. I rarely saw either one of them during my time in the field, except to look up at their command helicopters while they flew around directing our movements during firefights. Sometimes they would land their choppers after a firefight to look over the enemy equipment we captured. They were always the ones to pin medals on your fatigue shirt during award ceremonies.

Just north of Bong Son, at the end of a dirt road, was a tent city surrounded by concertina wire. This was LZ English. Each company in the field had its own tent back in the forward rear area, manned by a couple of infantry-men who were in charge of all the re-supply for the com-pany in the field. Usually, the guys in both the rear and forward rear area were short-timers or fellows who couldn't cut it in the field. The executive officer, the first sergeant, the supply sergeant and the company clerk were usually in the rear headquarters at An Khe. The forward rear area at LZ English was usually staffed by an NCO (non commis-sioned officer) who got help from guys who were on pro-file, those on sick call or had only a couple of days left in country. The brigade TOC (tactical operations center) and all the battalion TOCs were located nearby in underground bunkers that were sandbagged across the top. Detachments from the 227th Assault Helicopters (transport), the 228th

Aviation (Chinooks), and the 229th Assault (ARA) were stationed here with the 1st Brigade.

A brown-haired, blue-eyed sergeant named Rick Walker was at the company tent when we arrived. He was a short-timer with less than thirty days left in country, and he was in charge of the company rear area. He told us to stay close, we would be going out to join the company on the chow chopper around three p.m.

Everybody knew we were new guys. We had brand-new equipment, new fatigues and the camouflage covers on our steel helmets were spotless. Everybody avoided us like the plague. This was a peculiar practice of almost every guy I knew who put in a lot of time in the field—including me later on. When a new guy arrived in the field, almost everybody avoided him, refused to learn his name, until he had been around for a couple of months or until he proved himself under fire. A new guy had to earn the right to be admitted to the group's inner circle. The group might be the black guys, the white guys, the squad, the platoon, or the company. I've never quite figured it out, but I know it wasn't just the 1st Cav treating its new guys in this manner.

We boarded the re-supply and chow chopper mid-afternoon. I leaned forward in my seat and viewed some of the most spectacular scenery in the world. I couldn't believe there could be a war going on down there in such a beautiful setting. It looked so beautiful and peaceful from the air. I would soon learn the brutality and harshness of the terrain in the months to come. The hills were straight up and down and the level areas were covered with elephant grass higher than my head. Elephant grass would cut like razors when you brushed against it. When it rained, leeches were everywhere. They would latch on under your arms and between your legs. The only way to get them off was to burn them off with a cigarette or to squirt insect repellent directly on them. After they were removed, the spots where they had attached themselves bled and hurt like the dickens for a while. Snakes, gigantic bugs, and spiders were everywhere. But, the most danger below me was the enemy.

Under the Saigon government, Vietnam was divided into four Corps Tactical Zones, each commanded by a Vietnamese general for all the ARVN (Army of the Republic of Vietnam) forces within their assigned zone. From the DMZ (demilitarized zone) in the north at the 17th parallel, which was the border between North and South Vietnam, I Corps included all of Quang Ngai Province. Second Corps lay just below I Corps and included most of South Vietnam's Central Highlands. This was the AO (area of operations) for the 1st Cavalry Division. Third Corps lay further south and included the area to the west and north of Saigon. Fourth Corps is still further south and included the Mekong River Delta and Saigon.

NVA units infiltrated South Vietnam through the demilitarized zone at the 17th parallel and along the Ho Chi Minh Trail in Laos and Cambodia, a system of roads and foot trails meandering south before turning east toward the populated areas of South Vietnam. In addition to these NVA units, other Communist soldiers included the Viet Cong (VC) Main Force, District Force and Village Defense Force.

This VC Main Force was made up of VC shock troops composed of well-trained and equipped men who were capable of fighting conventional battles of limited duration. The District Force and Village Defense Force were made up of local civilians who were part-time soldiers, or guerrillas, whose military operations did not take them far from home. They were farmers and merchants during the day and terrorists at night. The less well trained were guides, guards, messengers, and informants for the regular military units.

The enemy, whether NVA or Viet Cong, were referred to as VC, "Victor Charlie" or just "Charlie." NVA units usually wore khakis and carried packs. The local guerrilla was clad in "calico noir," the traditional black pajamas of the peasants. The arms they carried ranged from 75 mm recoilless rifles, 82 mm, and 61 mm mortars to communist and French manufactured machine and submachine guns. Most had a few potato masher grenades. They were experts at camouflage and living and moving underground. Their elaborate tunnel complexes stretched sometimes for miles. They knew how to set ingenious booby traps, poisonous punji stakes, spike boards, Malaysian gates and trip-wire cross bows. A VC soldier usually weighed no more than one hundred pounds and subsisted on two pounds of rice a day.

His actions in battle have led some to suspect the use of narcotics before action, as reflected in this 1st Cav Operations report, 1965–1966:

"...they started charging me with 10 to 15 man waves, on a regular skirmish line, hollering and screaming. I hit some of them two or three times with bullets and they would keep coming at me, stop, turn around and then I could see big blood splotches on their backs as they took two or three steps toward their rear and then fell over. When they were charging me, they were yelling and even after I hit them with gunfire, they were laughing."

But I didn't know any of this yet. What I saw below was beautiful forest and jungle. It just didn't seem possible there was a war in such a remarkable place. I knew nothing of the history of the country, the people or the war effort.

DAY OF FIRSTS

The helicopter touched down on Hill 405, north and west of Bong Son in the Central Highlands. Hills and mountains in Vietnam are measured in meters. So this particular hill was 405 meters above sea level. We were only about eight to ten thousand meters west from the coast of the South China Sea. The day was May 25th.

Somebody took us to the company commander, Capt. Roland Parr. I don't remember much about the meeting. He welcomed us to the company and wished us well. I didn't know it at the time, but he had only about two weeks left in country before his DEROS (date estimated return overseas stateside). Larry Ashley did not accompany us to the field. They put him on some kind of detail work back in An Khe for a couple of days. He would join us in the 3rd platoon about a week later. Charlie Waskey and I were assigned to the 3rd platoon, Lt. John Rudd's platoon. I went to the first squad and Waskey was assigned to the weapons squad of the 3rd platoon. Even though Staff Sgt. Jennings was supposed to be squad leader of the first squad, he immediately became the platoon sergeant because he outranked the platoon sergeant. The next day, the battalion commander found out he was back in the field and ordered him back to the rear. Medal of Honor winners were normally banned from ever going back to the field. It wouldn't look good if a winner of our nation's highest award for bravery was captured and then broke under interrogation.

My new squad leader became Staff Sgt. Jesus Sablin, a native of Guam. He was absolutely a by-the-book guy. He talked down to everybody in his squad and never treated anybody with respect. He was an example of a poor leader. He tried to rule through intimidation and reminded me of my platoon sergeant in Germany, so I immediately disliked him. I made a mental note to myself, that if I ever became a sergeant, I would do everything the opposite of what I observed him doing. After chow, the assistant squad leader, Sgt. Richard Barry, another guy I grew to dislike, went through my backpack and threw out almost everything I had packed. I realized later that he did me a favor by removing all that extra weight. I made several other changes over the next few days, including throwing away my underwear. If a soldier wore underwear in the field, he would almost certainly develop jungle rot.

Just as it began to get dark, we saddled up with our equipment to move out. It was a common practice for the unit to move out after dark, relocate the company so the enemy could not register the new location in the daylight with their mortars or couldn't look over your perimeter to check for weak spots in the security.

We moved about two hundred yards. I could hear some of the veterans cursing some of the other new guys for being too noisy. We stopped, unloaded our backpacks, and set up for the night. I was in a three-man position for the night with Staff Sgt. Sablin and the other sergeant who had lightened my backpack. They gave me the first and fourth watches. Each watch would last about two hours. There was no moon out and my imagination ran wild, so that every bush and every tree concealed an enemy. I thought I saw several of the enemy advancing on my position. I woke Sablin up a couple of times to look out front of our position. He was a little cranky—as I was to become on a perpetual basis.

Imagine getting up at daybreak day after day and humping in the jungle or the mountains all day in blistering heat. You would come in, have chow, wait for dark, and move out to another position to pull guard for at least four hours or go outside the perimeter on ambush. Ambush patrol came every third night with 50 percent of the men on ambush awake during the night. Then the next two nights, we would pull regular guard duty with one guy awake in each foxhole or position at all times. You never got a good night's sleep. The only time this grind was interrupted was when you were in contact with the enemy or back in the rear area for "stand down." Stand down occurred when you came into a rear area that had showers and clean fatigues. We would shower and shave in cold water and then go hunt for a cold beer.

I made it through my first night in the field. The next morning I was exhausted. After we had a C ration breakfast, it was time to go on patrol. The SOP (standard operating procedures) for Charlie Company was much like the other companies in our battalion in the same AO. The 4th platoon, designated the weapons platoon, would set up their mortars and guard Capt. Parr's CP (Command Post), while the other three platoons would patrol out two thousand to three thousand meters or further on search and destroy missions. We didn't gripe much at the weapons platoon for getting light duty because they carried the mortar tubes, base plates, and mortar rounds every time we moved. They also were ready to provide the fire support we might need if we ran into the enemy.

The 1st Battalion had Headquarters, Alpha, Bravo, Charlie, and Delta companies. Headquarters Company included the cooks, supply people, truck drivers, communications personnel and medics. Most of those people were in the rear, with the exception of the medics. We usually had five medics assigned to us. One stayed with the company CP and each of the four platoons had its own. On any given day, one company would be doing "palace guard" on an LZ somewhere securing an artillery battery or two, while the other three companies would be out in their assigned AO's searching for the enemy. In this AO, our LZs were Geronimo, Laramie, X-Ray, Lowboy, and others whose names I don't remember. The artillery battery that supported us was usually B Battery, 2nd Battalion (Airborne), 19th Artillery. B Battery had been with Charlie Company on LZ Bird the previous December.

This was a day of firsts. It was my first patrol and my first day to walk point. I've heard other Vietnam veterans tell that their units never put new guys on point. Looking back on it now, I would say that since Lt. Rudd thought it was a relatively safe area, he decided to break me in faster. Or, it was probably that Staff Sgt. Sablin put me on point because I had disturbed his sleep the night before.

It was my first patrol and Lt. Rudd's last. He was from Florida, and from what I heard from the platoon, he was a first-rate officer and platoon leader. He could read a map correctly, even in the mountainous jungle, didn't take chances with his men, and made the platoon members live up to their responsibilities. We came down off the mountain on a finger and began our patrol. I took it slow, both watching the trail up ahead and looking down at my feet for booby traps. We traveled without flanks, something I thought was dangerous at the time. Putting out flanking squads or fire teams was noisy, slowed the main column down and was physically demanding on the flanks. But, patrolling with flanks kept the main column from walking into ambushes and taking heavy losses. Usually flanks flushed the enemy out before the main column walked into the killing zone.

We didn't see any enemy—VC or NVA. The intelligence briefing before our patrol had told of VC in the area operating with North Vietnamese regulars of the 22nd NVA Regiment. I discovered a few rice caches with about fifty pounds of grain in them. Lt. Rudd told me to scatter them as quickly as I could. We stopped there and checked the trails leading into the area, but failed to find any more signs of the enemy.

We arrived back at the CP, and I was relieved. I'd lived through my first day of operations. My spirits began to soar as I thought this might not be too bad. I might just live through this after all. I unbuckled my web gear, unloaded everything, took off my steel pot, and collapsed on top of my rucksack. For some reason, I looked off to a finger coming off an adjacent hill and spotted two heads under some bushes.

"Look over there! Are those guys ours?" I asked the guy next to me. He immediately began shouting, "Gooks! Gooks! On that finger at two o'clock!"

One of our machine gunners—Spec. 4th Class Tom Cusick of Lee's Summit, MO—picked up his M-60 machine gun, threw it in front of him, and lay down.

He screamed at his new ammo bearer, Charlie Waskey from Alaska, "Waskey, raise my legs! Raise my legs!" as loud as he could. He meant for Waskey to reach up to the adjustable bipod legs on the M-60 and move them up so he could use the bipods as a gun rest for more accurate firing at the two VC who were observing us. Waskey looked at Cusick like he was crazy, stood up, walked behind Cusick and picked up both his legs by his boots. All the guys watching burst out laughing.

Cusick said something like, "Not *my* legs, the legs on the gun!" By this time everybody was rolling on the ground with laughter. As we laughed hysterically, the two VC stood up and disappeared over the finger off the mountain into the brush. I pictured them saying to each other, "These crazy Americans are trying to laugh us to death!"

We had chow, waited for dark and moved another three hundred or four hundred meters to form our perimeter for the night. I didn't see as many of the enemy in the dark from our position while on guard that night. Such was the morning and evening of my first full day in the field. Sometime that evening, Lt. Radcliffe took over for Lt. Rudd. Rudd boarded the departing chow chopper, and that's the last time I saw him.

BAPTISM BY FIRE

The morning of May 27th broke as any other. It was hot and would get hotter. We had a C ration breakfast with a little coffee and saddled up with our equipment. I was glad I had walked point the previous day because I knew I wouldn't draw that assignment two days in a row. We moved out and my squad was in the middle of the column. Lt. Radcliffe was in the fourth man position.

Charlie Company patrols went with this formation: The point man was always out front about ten meters and behind him was one of the M-79 grenadiers. The M-79 guy was loaded with a HE (high explosive) round chambered, or if we were in heavy jungle, he would have a shotgun round. Next came the squad leader whose two men were in front of him. Behind him was the platoon leader followed by his RTO (radiotelephone operator) carrying a PRC-25 radio for radio transmission back to the CP. Right behind the RTO was the medic who was followed by the first machine gunner followed by the assistant gunner and the ammo bearer. The rest of the column followed them in no particular order until near the back came the other machine gun crew followed by the platoon sergeant and his RTO. The position of each gun allowed for the platoon leader and platoon sergeant to direct the placement of the M-60s in case of contact. After the platoon sergeant and RTO was another M-79 grenadier and the rear guard—or "back door man"—carrying an M-16. The only man allowed to be on full automatic was the point man. Everyone else could have a round chambered but had to have the safety on. Squad leaders were supposed to check each man's weapon before we moved out.

We patrolled all morning and formed a loose perimeter to take a break. I was seated, facing Lt. Radcliffe as he turned and gave the order, "Saddle up, let's move out!" His gaze went to the top of a small hill about seventy-five meters to our front where he spotted three VC or NVA watching us from their observation post. He shouted, "Gooks, gooks!" He pointed his CAR-15 at them and pulled the trigger. All he got was a *click*. He had forgotten to chamber a round.

We followed his line of sight to see the three VC stand up and run away from us down the little hill. Radcliffe shouted, "Line up and let's go after them!" I began running directly toward them, going through the draw that separated our position from the hill where we spotted the enemy soldiers. I fought the underbrush and broke out into a clearing. I suddenly realized I had outrun everyone in our platoon and was alone. Over to my right, I saw a lone grenadier named David Rowe emerge from the brush, and he moved by me to enter a break in the hedgerow in front of us. The hedgerow was on both sides of a little stream perhaps twenty feet across and about a foot deep.

Rowe stepped through the break in the hedgerow and into the stream. A burst of automatic weapons fire broke the silence. Rowe began backpedaling out of the stream as he yelled, "That gook shot at me!" He ran back about ten meters and got down on the ground. At that moment, the VC that had fired a burst at him began running down stream right in front of me. I moved forward and opened up on him with short bursts from my M-16. He stopped, swung the muzzle of his Thompson sub-machinegun toward me, and opened fire on me. I kept firing at him. I could see my rounds hitting him and chunks of flesh flying off his body behind him. He turned to his right and kept on running downstream out of my sight. I stood there in disbelief. I thought to myself, *These guys don't go down when you shoot them!*

When I regained my senses, I hit the dirt and saw Lt. Radcliffe had come up to my left.

He shouted at me, "What happened?"

"A gook ran downstream after he shot at us!"

He shouted, "Move downstream and throw a grenade!" I immediately ran to my left and hit the ground. I took a grenade, pulled the pin and threw it into the stream over the hedgerow, in order to pin the soldier down.

By then, the rest of the platoon had joined us. Lt. Radcliffe and a couple of us got on line and went through the hedgerow and into the stream. We looked up and down the stream and saw nobody. Someone pointed at a stick that protruded up out of the stream. Radcliffe immediately fired into the stream on full automatic with his CAR-15. The water turned red. I couldn't figure out what he was shooting. He reached down into the stream and pulled out a VC soldier who had been breathing through a bamboo tube. His whole underside was gushing blood.

I moved down the stream a bit and found the soldier I had confronted earlier lying on his stomach half out of the stream. I pushed on him with my M-16, and he grunted. I turned him over, careful to keep his body as a shield in case he had a live grenade underneath him. I had hit him several times. Radcliffe ran up, sized up the situation, and told me to move upstream to see if there were any others.

I moved out and began my recon upstream. I noticed I was shaking like a leaf as I was slowly, carefully looking out for any other VC that might be hiding about. I happened to look down at my weapon and realized I had no magazine in my rifle. I was looking for armed VC and I had one round in my M-16! I quickly loaded another magazine in my rifle and checked to see that I had a round chambered. I had failed to ensure that my magazine was firmly seated in my rifle when I reloaded earlier, and it had fallen out. It was my first stupid mistake; I never made that one again. Fortunately, I didn't encounter any other enemy personnel.

I heard gunfire downstream. The rest of the platoon had found the other VC. By the time I got back to where I had left the two bodies, the guys had dragged the body of the third VC to the area. We had three VC with one Thompson sub-machinegun and two AK-47s. I heard the command chopper in the distance and watched as Lt. Col. Riddlehoover's chopper landed.

He got a report from Lt. Radcliffe, looked over the bodies and remarked, "Good job, men!" He got back on his helicopter with the captured weapons and took off. Our medic had administered first aid to the one VC still alive, but he died before we could get a medevac for him.

Someone yelled, "Break for chow," and we sat down for a while in a perimeter position.

I looked over at the dead VC bodies and felt sick at my stomach. I had no appetite whatsoever. I had just killed a man. On several occasions, I've had people ask me flat out how it felt to kill the enemy in Vietnam. I don't think I've ever answered anyone truthfully. The truth is it makes you feel rotten. Looking back on the experience, I never got any thrill out of taking another human being's life, even when I killed people who were trying to kill me. One minute a guy is breathing, the next he's dead, forever. I have never felt good about the killing. The only way I've justified it to myself is that I was in the process of self-preservation. I became a very aggressive soldier when I was in Vietnam. There were many times I confronted the enemy up close, and I was faster. But I didn't revel in shooting the enemy. It just happened, and I'm still here. For this action, I was put in for a Bronze Star with "V" device (Valor device identifies the award as resulting from combat heroism), though I don't know by whom or when the recommendation was made.

So began and ended my second full day in combat in Vietnam. My feelings the day before that I might just make it were gone. Instead I thought, *If the rest of my tour is like these first two days, it doesn't look good for me.* Something changed that day, though. I noticed that the old veterans in the platoon began treating me differently. Guys kept coming over to me, introducing themselves and even using my name when they talked to me. I had been inducted into "the guys." I was a keeper. I hadn't folded under fire. Now I was one of them, and I liked it. As time went on, I would form the closest relationships of my life. These were "the guys" who would come out under fire to get you if you were hit, share their last cigarette with you, loan you anything they had, and tell you the most intimate details about their lives. It's an experience I miss to this day.

RADIO OPERATOR

The next couple of days are a blur to me. It was three more days of patrolling, pulling guard at my position and moving after dark. I did another very dumb thing during this time. I went to sleep after we got back from one of our day patrols and was inside our perimeter. When I dropped off, I was lying on my back on my backpack under a shade tree. A little later, I lost the shade and was out in the sun snoozing away. I am a mouth breather and my mouth was wide open while I was sleeping. I sunburned the roof of my mouth. It was so bad I spit lining from the roof of my mouth for several days. It was not the last stupid thing I did.

Somewhere around this time, I experienced my first air assault. One morning, we were picked up by the 227th Aviation choppers from the 1st Cav. The helicopters came in seven at a time for us to load. The only thing said to me that I remember was, "Don't forget to duck when you run to load on the choppers." I think that advice is self-explanatory. We flew down to the Bong Son Plain near Highway 1. Highway 1 was a dirt road that ran through rice paddies near the coast the entire length of Vietnam. We touched down on the LZ near a village and quickly surrounded it. While one platoon formed a blocking force on the backside of the village, the rest of us formed a line and went through the village searching all the houses. The search was uneventful.

We later grouped around a stream just outside the village. The water was clear and cold. Somebody produced a bar of soap, and we took turns taking a bath. It was my first bath in over a week. It was a welcome relief from the horrendous heat, at least for a couple of moments.

I also remember that on one of those nights I went on my first ambush. After chow, we stowed all our equipment that might make unnecessary noise with the rest of the platoon. This was to be a squad-sized ambush party with an attached machine gun team. We took off in the dark and moved down a mountain trail about three hundred meters. We moved off the trail and Staff Sgt. Daniel Rozzelle put us in groups of two up over the trail. At the very end of the ambush line, he positioned the M-60 gun facing out toward the trail. We had formed the classic L-shaped ambush. I don't remember who my partner was at my position, but I do know I was awake exactly half the night.

Someone manning the radio answered the call for a situation report called a "sit-rep" every hour by mashing the button on the radio handset to break squelch. When the handset is depressed, it silenced the static on the other end of the transmission and assured the company radio operator that all was well without any verbal acknowledgement. We had to be absolutely quiet. It's not a good feeling with seven guys in your squad and three men on the machine gun so far from the rest of the company. We made it through the night without incident. Then it was back to the company perimeter for breakfast and back to the grind of patrolling the next day.

I began to form friendships with the other guys in our platoon. I was drawn to Tom Cusick, one of our machine gunners, from Lees Summit, Missouri. Tom had been with Charlie Company since the previous September. His gun crew consisted of him, his assistant gunner, Rick Boeshart and ammo bearer, Charlie Waskey. I was also drawn to "Bo" (or Boeshart) and Waskey. They were easy to get along with.

If you had asked SSG Rozelle his opinion of Tom Cusick, his response would have been that Cusick was insolent and a trouble maker, with a bad attitude. For some reason, unknown to me, Cusick and Rozelle were like oil and water. If Rozelle gave Cusick an order, Tom made it a point to question it. Rozelle, a black man, had been in the army for several years and was an "old school" paratrooper. He was Ranger qualified and was a master parachutist. He did not like draftees and Tom Cusick was a draftee. Tom told me several stories about how it was when the first non airborne personnel like him came to the field. He said that Rozelle and several of the airborne guys would kick and hit the new non airborne guys or "legs" when they couldn't keep up the pace on patrol.

The next three days and nights stand out very clearly in my memory. On the afternoon of May 30th, we hastily beat a path back to the company area after a call from Capt. Parr. After our return, my platoon moved a short distance to secure an LZ for Riddlehoover's chopper. I found myself standing next to Lt. Radcliffe.

He spoke in his usual brisk, New England way, "Warden, I've been watching you. You are doing a good job. My RTO is leaving tonight for R&R and then back to the States. How would you like to carry my radio? It will get you off guard duty, ambush, and listening post. All you have to do is keep me in contact over the radio and make sure I get C rations every day." How could I turn down a deal like that? I thanked him and quickly accepted.

I hurriedly took the PRC-25 radio from Eddie Fain, the departing RTO. He showed me how to adjust my backpack down to accommodate the radio, told me my call sign was Smoking Barrel Three-Six India, and Lt. Radcliffe was Smoking Barrel Three-Six. That was as much training as I was going to get on radio procedures. Fain called good luck to me as he boarded the chopper with the colonel to return to the rear.

I was now the RTO for the 3rd platoon leader. I was desperately trying to remember my radio training and the phonetic alphabet from my advanced infantry training. Call signs became a way of identifying the company commander, platoon leaders, and sergeants as well as the RTOs. Smoking Barrel Six was the company commander, One-Six was the 1st platoon leader, Two-Six was the 2nd platoon leader and so on. One-Six Mike was the 1st platoon sergeant and so on. I was Smoking Barrel Three-Six India. All the RTOs were identified by their assigned leader's call sign followed by the phonetic alphabet indicator "India," except for the guys who carried the radios for the platoon sergeants. They used Alpha. For instance, the radio guy for Three-Six Mike was Three-Six Alpha.

Ten minutes later, as dusk was approaching, we got the order to assemble at the LZ for a night air assault. Elements of the 22nd NVA regiment had been in contact with one of our sister companies late in the day. We were flying in to be a blocking force on the Bong Son Plain.

We boarded the helicopters in the dark. We could only load one chopper at a time, so the loaded choppers circled overhead until two platoons were loaded. Then, it was off

to the Bong Son Plain near the village of An Qui 1. We
flew at an altitude of about two thousand feet. It's strange
that the surface distance was measured in meters and the
air distance was measured in feet. Guess it was because all
the old French-made maps we had were in meters. Anyway,
I was sitting in the seat next to the open door with Lt.
Radcliffe in front of me with his feet dangling out of the
helicopter. As we approached the landing zone, we could
see green-colored tracers directed our way. He knew every
sixth round was a tracer for night firing. They curved away
from us and passed harmlessly behind us.

Radcliffe turned to me and said, "Doug, those are NVA
tracer rounds; ours are red." At that moment, you could not
have driven a small nail through my sphincter muscle with
a sledgehammer.

We hit the ground, in the dark and formed a 360-degree
perimeter to wait for the rest of the company. After they
arrived, our platoon moved out about 1,500 meters to join
up with a platoon of tanks. We moved east and south to
establish a blocking position east of the village of Thanh
Son 1. The NVA had ambushed a squad from one of our
sister battalions. We walked in full field packs in soft, white
sand. By the time we arrived, I was exhausted.

We formed a perimeter with a few waiting tanks in
the dark. Lt. Radcliffe, and I ended up in between two
tanks that had their gun turrets pointed across the sand
toward a line of palm trees about two hundred meters away.
Radcliffe gave me the first radio watch. There was a furrow that ran between the tanks. It looked like someone had
plowed it. I positioned my backpack on the edge of it, sat
down with my butt in the furrow, and leaned back against
my pack. I put the headset for the radio up against my ear

and promptly dozed off. This was the unforgivable sin of the infantryman in combat. Going to sleep on guard jeopardized everybody in company. My only defense was that I was still a new guy, but that's no excuse.

A tremendous explosion woke me. I saw a gigantic ball of fire in front of me and felt sparks on my face. The first thing that entered my mind was that we were being attacked. I picked up the headset and began shouting into the microphone, "Six, Six, this is Three-Six India. We're being mortared! We're being mortared!"

Someone at the company CP answered and began to ask for my situation. I was confused and frightened beyond belief. A hand reached over my shoulder and took the handset. It was Lt. Radcliffe. He got on the phone and told the captain I had mistaken a round from the tank beside us as incoming mortar fire.

Then he turned to me, "Jesus Christ, Warden, don't you know the difference between friendly outgoing fire and incoming?" I didn't, and I couldn't even speak. While I was dozing, one of the tankers had spotted movement out to our front with his infrared scope and opened fire with his cannon. I was really ashamed of myself. I never told anybody I had gone to sleep on my watch. It was another dumb thing that I never did again.

The next morning we moved out to a position about one thousand meters south and east of An Qui 1 village. As we walked past the CP and the company radio operators, they catcalled to me in really high-pitched voices, "Six, Six, this is Three-Six India. We're being mortared! We're being mortared!" I could have died right where I stood. All of the respect I had gained was now gone. Everyone had a laugh at my expense as we had C ration coffee. I felt about one inch tall.

RIDE INTO HELL

The 3rd platoon loaded up on two tanks to ride out to begin a fishhook maneuver toward a village nearby. We had been north of An Qui 1 the night before, so we moved south to east to north and crossed the bridge to An Qui 1 from the south.

I looked back and saw our guys jumping off the tanks. But after they had jumped, they weren't getting up and running. Then I heard the cry from someone, "Incoming rounds! Get off the tanks!" Our platoon was in the middle of a dry rice paddy, one hundred meters from the village of An Qui 1, and taking heavy fire from every direction. There were thirty of us, and we were facing an estimated two hundred NVA. Our medic that day was SP4 Jack Barrett. He was a busy man the rest of the day. Spec. 4th Class Walter Gutson from New Jersey and Spec. 4th Class Bill Moder from St. Louis were among those who had been shot off the tanks. We had two other wounded up in front of me.

I found myself lying in the sand next to a sergeant named Bill Money. I was looking at him, thinking it was strange I had never seen him before today even though we were in the same platoon, when he attempted to speak to me. His eyes rolled back in his head, and he dropped face first, into the sand. I crawled to him and rolled him over. I felt his neck artery and looked at his lifeless eyes. He was dead. It was the first time I ever witnessed an American soldier dying. I was stunned and speechless. Later, some of the guys suggested that the rounds he took were meant for me because I had a radio on my back.

Lt. Radcliffe crawled up to me in the sand and got on the radio to contact Capt. Parr and apprise him of our situation. He got off the radio and asked the guys around us if they were hit. Several cried out that they couldn't walk or run. He turned to those of us who weren't hit and told us to spread out. I looked toward the nearest tank. It was manned by one of the best soldiers I've ever met, Staff Sgt. Chuck Hazelip of A Company, 1st Battalion, 69th Armor.

Hazelip, a native of Kentucky, opened the hatch and told us he was going to attack the positions in front of him. Hazelip was shirtless, since it was very hot inside the tank. We got on line with his tank and moved forward, firing as we walked and ran. Hazelip was firing every few seconds into the bunkers in front of us. Suddenly two RPG (rocket propelled grenade) rounds passed through us, meant for his tank. One round hit a mound with trees over to my left, and the shrapnel hit Staff Sgt. Sablin and Sgt. Barry, the sergeant who had gone through my pack my first night in the field.

Sablin got up and kept on going toward a hole underneath a palm tree. Every so often, an NVA soldier would pop up from that hole and spray us with automatic rifle fire. I started toward the hole to drop a grenade in it, when the NVA soldier threw a grenade toward me. It landed right between my feet. You've heard accounts of critical situations making time stand still? Time stopped right there for me. I saw that it was a ChiCom grenade, a tin can filled with explosives attached to a wooden handle. I gathered all my muscles to jump and just started to leap when it went off. The blast carried me a good three feet in the air, and I rolled another six feet. My legs and arms were burning like fire. Without realizing it, I had put one hand down between my legs to protect my testicles. Even though I was sprayed with hot metal and bleeding from where a couple of the larger pieces had hit, I could still move and function.

Sablin had crawled forward and dropped a grenade down the hole. It came right back out and we scrambled for cover. Hazelip drove forward, barely missed by another RPG round. He buried the muzzle of his cannon in the hole of the pesky NVA and blew dirt thirty feet in the air. Scratch one bad guy. I got a call from Capt. Parr for Lt. Radcliffe, and I hurried over to him to give him the handset. Parr told him to pull back from the village, that an ARA ship was going to strafe the village. While Radcliffe was talking to the captain, he went down suddenly. He was shot in the neck. I got on the radio and reported to Capt. Parr, "My Six has been hit!" Lt. Radcliffe got to his feet, took the radio handset back, and resumed talking to the company commander. Radcliffe was in charge again! I immediately felt better knowing that Lt. Radcliffe was OK. If something happened to him, we would be in even more serious trouble than what we were in. The Lieutenant was managing every aspect of our defense. He placed all of us in whatever cover he could find.

When we pulled back about fifty meters and took all our wounded, we realized we were down to eight guys who could walk and function. Walter Gutson had crawled up on the back tank and banged on the lid. When it opened, he crawled inside with the crew. He had lost his weapon, and it seemed like the logical thing to do at the time. He stayed inside the tank until he was medevaced.

Radcliffe gathered about six of us, including Tom Cusick, our machine gunner, Rick Boeshart, the assistant gunner from Sioux Falls, Iowa, the ammo bearer, Charley Waskey, and David Wilkowski, an M-79 grenadier, to make an assault on the right side of the village in an attempt to take the withering fire off of us and our comrades. Another machine gunner named LeRoy Burgess went with us. We assaulted about one hundred meters into the village and found ourselves in the middle of an NVA force of about thirty soldiers. They were dug in, manning slit trenches, and firing at us from the entrances of several bunkers. One of our guys was hit, and we dragged him out with us, back to our wounded in the middle of the sandy rice paddy.

Radcliffe was quietly cursing to himself and turned to me and said, "Warden, grab every grenade you can and get ready to come with me!" He had an idea to reverse the fire superiority of the enemy. I got about eight or nine grenades to add to the four that I was carrying and stuck them down my shirt and got up with Radcliffe to follow him into the village.

Now I was six-foot-three and 150 pounds, but Radcliffe towered over me. He was six-foot-five and weighed around 190. We were big targets, plus I was still wearing the radio on my back for his communications with the company commander.

We ran toward the center of the village and lay down next to the bunker complex. I took out a grenade while Radcliffe covered my back. I pulled the pin and reached around from the side of the bunker to throw the grenade into it. A face appeared in the doorway. I don't know who was more surprised, him or me. I didn't give him any time to react. I hit him in the center of the forehead with the butt of the grenade and knocked him back. Then I tossed in the grenade. Erase one or more bad guys.

We got to the next bunker, and I tossed my grenade in, and it came right back out. We scrambled to get away from it. It's one thing to get hit by an inferior ChiCom grenade, but it's another to be near an American-made grenade when it goes off. They will absolutely kill you dead if you are within five to six feet. Even at ten feet away, you'll be seriously wounded. We crawled back up to the bunker. Lt. Radcliffe threw one in, and it came back out, but I heaved mine, and it stayed in the hole. I guess the guy inside couldn't handle two at once. We scrambled away again from our first grenade as it went off harmlessly. Scratch more bad guys. We probably spent twenty to thirty minutes in there by ourselves. We ran out of grenades and retreated back out to our wounded. Our little excursion had worked, though. The enemy rounds directed our way diminished considerably.

We got a call on the radio that artillery was on the way and to pull back as soon as we could. We got the tanks over to us, loaded the wounded on top, and walked back to the bridge we had crossed coming in; then we got in the dry creek bed. It was at this time that a lone American soldier joined us. He was from the 8th Engineer Battalion. He had been doing some construction work nearby and had been surrounded with us. He had fought against the enemy all by himself. He caught a re-supply chopper a little later, and I never saw him again. I never heard what his name was, but he should have been given some recognition for his efforts to help us out that day.

We watched as perhaps two hundred or three hundred artillery rounds began pounding the village in front of us. A little while later, other tanks and the rest of our company joined us in the dry streambed. We had been in heavy contact with the enemy until the late afternoon. Radcliffe later told me that by performing the fishhook maneuver, we had driven up to the enemy's command post. We had destroyed their command post that afternoon.

Medevac helicopters began transporting our wounded and Sgt. Bill Money's body out. The rest of the company had taken some time to get to us, since they didn't have tanks to transport them. Lt. Norm Mordue's 2nd platoon attacked from west to east to take some of the pressure off us. He lost two KIAs (killed in action) and four WIAs (wounded in action), including himself. Over thirty of us had been in the 3rd platoon that morning; now there were only seven left. I looked around at Cusick, Boeshart, and Waskey. For the first time, I saw the "thousand yard stare." It is a faraway look men get when they search for the enemy in the distance and have been within an inch of death and scared to death. I guess I looked the same to them. My friendships with these guys only deepened after what we had gone through together. As time went on, we became like brothers.

We spent the night as part of a containment force with the trapped enemy force. It was that night I saw Snoopy fire on the enemy for the first time. Snoopy was an old C-47 (DC-3) armed with mini-guns and Gatling guns. Every sixth round was a tracer, and it looked like a steady stream of red fire beneath the fuselage going toward the enemy forces below. It was said that Snoopy could fire for a minute and put one round in every square inch of an area the size of a football field. I'm glad I was on our side that night. The tenacity and bravery of the NVA soldiers always amazed me. They were ill equipped, fed on rice, treated in primitive hospitals, had no armor or air support, but they didn't run.

The next morning, I witnessed the assault by our other three platoons into the village from a streambed behind the assault force. The 3rd platoon didn't participate because we had only seven guys left, including Lt. Radcliffe. They got on line, stood up, and walked forward firing as they went. Two more of our guys were killed. In all, Charlie Company lost six including Sgt. Money. We had over thirty wounded. The enemy left ninety-eight dead behind when it was all over.

Up front of us, Charles Fletcher and John Spencer were with the weapons platoon. Fletcher told me that one of the platoon sergeants, who was trying to get in some field time to get a promotion, was behind them. Spencer advanced to a well that had a large, round board covering the top of it. He took his M-16 barrel and raised the lid to look under it for anyone who might be hiding inside. After he was satisfied there was no one in the well, he let the board drop back with a bang. The platoon sergeant got spooked and fired his M-16 on full automatic toward Spencer. Though he emptied the magazine in his M-16, he missed hitting Spencer. He was gone that afternoon, never to return to the field.

In all, the morning assault lasted about an hour. Capt. Parr hunkered down in the protected streambed and directed the assault from there. I thought his actions were odd after witnessing what Lt. Radcliffe had done the day before, putting himself in harm's way by directing his men from the battlefield and taking fire with them. But I was just a private first class, and what I thought, I kept to myself. I know we kicked a numerically superior force right in the teeth over the course of two days. All during that time, I never saw anyone run or refuse to follow an order. I knew then that I was with a first class fighting outfit.

The support we got from the artillery and gunships had been superb. One thing about the Cav, they supplied and supported their fighting men in the best way. Every day about three o'clock, we got a hot meal and re-supply, unless we were in heavy jungle or in contact. When we were in a battle, the choppers would come in, hover over us, and kick out ammunition and water on top of us while drawing heavy fire. While I'm thinking about it, I will mention something strange that always occurred to me when we were in a firefight. Every time we were in heavy contact, I started out with full canteens. But when the firing was over, I was always out of water, and I never remember taking a drink during the fighting. Strange how things like that happen without any memory of them.

So ended my first week in the field. For this action, eight men in our company received the Silver Star, our country's third highest award for "gallantry in action" as the award reads. I was one of them. Sgt. Chuck Hazelip, the tank commander attached to our platoon, and Lt. Norm Mordue were awarded the Distinguished Service Cross for their actions. Our company was later awarded the Valorous Unit Citation, the equivalent of the Silver Star for everyone in Charlie Company. After the end of my first week, I was even more confident I would never see Prague, OK, again. Fifty-one more weeks of what I had just gone through was more than I could possibly survive.

The afternoon of June 1st, I got on a medevac flight out of the An Qui 1 area to go back to Bong Son where the 15th Medical Battalion was located. I needed treatment for the fragment cuts I had received the previous day. I was treated with some antibiotics and bandages. The next day, I went downtown with some of the guys who were returning from the field. I bought a waterproof watch from a street vendor for ten dollars. I waded out into the Bong Son River and watched the face of the watch fill up with water and stop the second hand. I turned around to look for the street vendor, but he was nowhere to be seen. So much for "waterproof" watches bought in downtown Bong Son city.

But, I never again heard anyone refer to my stupid radio transmission to the captain about "the mortar attack" that was really friendly fire. On June 2nd, they gave us laundered fatigues to replace the ones we had been wearing for over a week for an impact award ceremony, as well as a memorial service for the six men we had lost at An Qui 1. Lieutenant Radcliffe received the Silver Star that day. He more than deserved it. I am convinced he should have received the Distinguished Service Cross for what I saw him do.

The memorial service was sad beyond belief. The jungle boots and helmets lined up in remembrance of our fallen comrades brought tears to my eyes. I vowed never again to attend a memorial service after that day, and I never did. The ceremony was for Pfc. Hervey H. Harris, Sgt. Teddy

R. Dunn, Sgt. Bill W. Money, Sgt. Dennie Nease, Pfc. James E. Rickerson, and Pfc. Jerald A. Vokish.

Most of the 4th platoon came over to become members of the 3rd platoon. Among these soldiers were Charles Fletcher, John Spencer and Cliff Metz.

PART III:
SEARCH AND DESTROY

DEATH AND CARNAGE

The next day, it was back out to the field to begin operations again. I don't remember much about the next week, but I do remember June 9th. We were quite a ways north of Bong Son and east of Highway 1 checking out a series of bombed out villages that were located almost on the shoreline of the South China Sea. The terrain was rolling hills in sand that was extremely hard to walk through. One of our machine gun teams from the weapons squad was over to the right of Lt. Radcliffe and me.

The weapons squad leader was a specialist 4th class who had just come to the Cav from another infantry unit in Vietnam, because we were woefully short of non commissioned officers to lead squads and platoons. I believe he told me he had just nine days left in country before he was slated to go home. His name was Spec. 4th Class Sam Durham from Lomita, CA. The machine gunner was Rufus Ray, a black guy from Odessa, Texas, and the assistant gunner was another black guy named Jim Johnson from Gilmer, Texas. The ammo bearer was Larry Ashley, my newfound friend I had met at the Oakland Army Terminal before we flew to Vietnam. Ashley had arrived in the field just after our firefight at An Qui. I was elated to see him again. We talked about what had happened during our firefight. He was glad, in a way, to have missed the firefight, but a part of him also wanted to have been there. He was anxious to have his "baptism of fire" and earn his Combat Infantry Badge. He hadn't been in Vietnam long enough to get a letter from his wife, Dixie. I could tell that he was homesick already. I was already so homesick that tears came into my eyes every time I thought of home. I was pretty sure that I would never see home again, though I didn't mention this to Ashley. Anyway, it was good to have Ashley in the same platoon as me and I told him so.

As we passed through a completely razed village, Spec. Durham used his rifle to raise a detached wooden door to look under it. Ray, Johnson and Ashley were all around him, watching as he raised the door. Under the door was a booby-trapped, unexploded 155 mm howitzer round. It exploded, shredding about forty-five pounds of jagged steel and sending it toward the four men at near supersonic speed. Durham was slammed to the ground with the force of the blast and never moved after that. He was one of the lucky ones. Ray was also killed immediately. Johnson screamed for over fifteen minutes until he died. Ashley was mad from the moment he hit the ground. The booby trap had blown off his right leg above the knee, and the other leg was hanging on by a piece of muscle. Ashley was screaming, "Why the hell did this have to happen to me?" None of us had the answer to his question. We could only look on, dumbfounded!

Doc Leroy worked on Johnson and Ashley as fast as he could. He gave both of them shots of morphine, but it did no good for Johnson—he started losing the battle for his life within minutes. Ashley was alive when we put him on the medevac helicopter. I accompanied the stretcher that held him, carrying his boot with part of his leg still in it. After the helicopter raced away, I stumbled back to my radio and sat down. I couldn't believe all the death and carnage that was caused by the hidden enemy. We hadn't been able to fire a shot, yet we had three dead and one seriously wounded.

I couldn't imagine how Ashley would ever make it. Ashley had been in country less than twenty days, and he was already going home with less than a whole body. I was stunned by this event. I got very little sleep that night. I kept hearing Johnson's screams and kept seeing Ashley as he was writhing in pain and cursing in the sand. I could remember watching as they loaded Durham, Johnson, and Ray on the helicopter for their last ride. I fought back the tears of utter despair, knowing I could have been like Ashley or one of the dead. Ashley had been the first friend I made in Vietnam, and I felt a great sense of loss.

A couple of days later, we were in the same area working with some tanks that were sweeping the area because of the number of booby traps. I happened to be looking down at the ground, and I saw what appeared to be a piece of fishing line stretched across the sand. I immediately grabbed Lt. Radcliffe by the back of his fatigue shirt and yanked on him to stop. I pointed down at the catgut line. Radcliffe followed the line to the right. It was hooked to a mousetrap device attached to the firing mechanism on an unexploded 155 mm round. The same thing that happened to our comrades just a couple of days before had almost happened to Radcliffe and me. We were extremely lucky. Lieutenant Radcliffe called for some engineers to come out and look at it. It was fully armed and ready to go off. They exploded it in place. There was one whale of an explosion. Lieutenant Radcliffe and I were two lucky soldiers.

Over the next twenty days, we probably participated in twelve to fifteen air assaults. Sometimes we would make two or three a day. This was done to confuse the enemy. It was also done for the surprise effect it had on their operations. On one hot day, the battalion commander had us climbing a high mountain in the Central Highlands just over from the Bong Son Plain. It was steep, and we were in full field gear. I was carrying about eighty pounds with a full field pack and PRC-25 radio. Col. Riddlehoover was circling around and around the top of the mountain in his helicopter. I think it was around 115 F. We medevaced five or six men due to heat-related injuries.

One private from Detroit named Tom Corey suffered a heat stroke. We had to mix up mud with our canteen water to cool him down. We carried him down the mountain and put him on the chopper. I never did find out what was so important that we should scale that mountain under full combat load with the temperature soaring. I do remember Lt. Radcliffe telling the battalion commander he would not take us up that mountain again. They argued over the radio, but Radcliffe prevailed. That was one of the reasons we revered him so much. He looked out for his guys.

One afternoon, our company was airlifted by helicopter to an LZ south of Bong Son. We got hot chow, showered, and changed clothes. There were three fifty-five-gallon drums full of beer on ice. We continued drinking beer into the evening. Around eight o'clock, we ran out of beer, and we really were feeling the alcohol. I don't remember whose idea it was, but someone suggested we go out the gate to find some Tiger 33, the local Vietnamese beer. We knew there would be a few bars right outside the gate. We also knew no one would allow us to do that.

So, I drew lieutenant bars on my fatigues with an ink pen and organized the guys into something that looked like a real patrol. There were several of us in on this conspiracy. Tom Cusick, Phillip "Tyke" Hayes, Cliff Metz, Calvin Gouley, Rich Valles, David Wilkowski, and some others loaded their weapons and put on their web gear. We marched up to the gate in single file. I addressed the MP on guard at the gate and told him we were going on a patrol. He let us through without question and with a salute, which I returned smartly. We went two hundred to three hundred yards outside the wire, knocking on doors and asking occupants for anything containing alcohol. We were unsuccessful, so we returned to the LZ and promptly went into an alcohol-induced sleep. At four a.m., we were awakened to go on a cordon mission. The idea of a cordon mission was for a sizable force of infantry to surround a village and wait for the Vietnamese National Police (we called them "white mice" because of their white helmets and gloves) to come in and interrogate all the occupants. Those of us who had been drinking the night before were still drunk. I couldn't even stand on the trail. Lieutenant Radcliffe had to hold on to me to keep me from falling. He wasn't happy with me and gave me a piece of his mind the next morning, but he didn't turn any of us in. We moved down to the village and took up our positions. Radcliffe told me to go to sleep after we got set up. When I woke up, the Vietnamese police had about twenty people seated in front of us. Some of them had bandages on various parts of their bodies. We had surrounded a village where there was a VC hospital. I looked around and discovered that we were at the same place where we had knocked on doors the night before. Another stupid stunt I lived through, and something else I never repeated.

FRIEND AND MENTOR

We spent the next couple of weeks near an abandoned schoolhouse north of Bong Son doing search and destroy missions. We would locate bunkers and use C-4 explosives to destroy them. The bunkers were made by the civilian population to protect themselves from American artillery and helicopter gunfire, but the VC and NVA sometimes would use the bunkers to hide in to escape our artillery. C-4 was a plastic explosive we could stick next to a support beam inside the bunker and explode, thereby destroying the bunker by blowing off the top of it.

It was much the same every day for a while, until around the second or third week of June when we were hastily picked up by helicopters and transported to the airport at LZ English. We drew extra ammo and maps. The maps were of the Sinai Peninsula. The Six-Day War between Egypt and Israel had begun. I was never sure what light infantry was supposed to do to intervene in the war, but it was unsettling just the same. Lt. Radcliffe was pretty calm about the whole affair. His stated position on going to the Sinai Peninsula was, "By the time we get there, the tank war will be over. All we will be used for is security." Since he was so confident that we would be safe if we were deployed, we all felt better. We stayed at LZ English on standby for about three days until the war was over. Israel destroyed the Egyptian army in a six-day time span. I was glad Israel took care of business rather quickly.

It was during this time that I met Larry Register from Alabama and Stan Tunall from California. They were both in the 1st platoon. Tunall was the RTO for Lt. Lentsch and Register was one of the guys in the 1st platoon. One day when we were using a schoolhouse as our command post, Register threw a grenade into a bunker about seventy or eighty yards from where I was sitting. A piece of shrapnel flew out of the opening of the bunker and hit me square in the back. It had enough force to knock me down and hurt a lot, though it didn't break the skin. Some guys gathered around me to help out and Register and Tunall came over to see what was going on. Register apologized for the accident. There was really no reason for him to apologize; it was a freak accident. After our meeting, Tunall and I started a little game whenever we talked to each other on the radio. We would follow strict radio procedure and spell out most everything using the phonetic alphabet; "Roger, wait!" and "Roger, Wilco!" for example. The truth is, I learned a lot about how to communicate over the radio from Stan Tunall.

I had gained enough respect from the guys who had been there for awhile to become part of the group. Tom Cusick had the most time in-country, so we hung around with him. When we took a break or were waiting for the chow chopper to show up, we all congregated together. Tom was about 5 foot, 8 inches tall with dark brown hair. He was born and raised in Lees Summit, Missouri. He enjoyed country and western music, telling us war stories about LZ

Bird and 506 Valley and beer. Most every day, we would get a can of hot beer with our evening meal about 4 o'clock. Most of us couldn't drink hot beer, but Cusick could. So, he always ended up with an extra can or two most every day. Cusick was easy to like. He was a draftee with a family back home. He had two little girls that were being raised by his wife, Sharon. He was a terrible garrison soldier in the rear. He would always question why we had to pull any details that came along from our sergeants. And, when we were pulling details, he was always the slowest worker. But, when we were in the field and drew fire, he was the first one to charge toward where the bullets were coming from to deliver accurate fire from his M-60 machine gun. He only had a couple of months left in the army and was close to going home, but we became fast friends. He told me that he liked me because I didn't act conceited as Radcliffe's RTO. I think he also liked me because, like him, I would try to get up front to where the action was. I really didn't have any choice, because Radcliffe was a leader who led from the front and as his RTO, I had to be within a arm's length of him with his radio.

So, when we came in from the field to an LZ, Tom Cusick, Rick Boeshart, Charlie Waskey, Cliff Metz, Calvin Gouley, David Wilkowski, Billy Cabaniss, Luis Vincente, Dennis Rasmussen, Rich Valles and Phillip Hayes would always be congregated somewhere talking about home, girlfriends, wives, kids, cars, etc. and always looking for a beer.

On June 20th, we air assaulted to a village in the Bong Son Plain, north of Bong Son city. As we started to enter the village, we drew heavy automatic weapons fire. Our company commander called in artillery. Lieutenant Radcliffe and I sat behind a mound of dirt with several of our platoon waiting for the rounds to cease. We knew when the artillery stopped, we would saddle up and get on line to do an assault, just like I had witnessed in An Qui.

I tried not to worry about what was going to happen, but I didn't have much to say to anybody.

I turned to Radcliffe and said, "Sir, if anything happens to either one of us today, I just wanted you to know that it has been an honor to be your RTO."

Radcliffe looked at me and replied, "You're pretty special to me too, Warden. I think we'll make it through just fine, but if one of us doesn't, let's contact our folks to let them know what happened." I really don't know why we were so sentimental. Facing death does funny things to men, even brave guys like Radcliffe. Notice I didn't mention my name as being associated with being brave. At that time, I was what I would call a victim of circumstance. I was just hanging out with brave men.

The artillery stopped. We stood up and began our sweep through the village. We hadn't gone fifty meters when we came upon a woman and a little girl lying where they had been killed. I don't know whether the artillery got them, the VC shot them, or if we got them with small arms fire. We moved on through the village without any return fire. VC had a habit of taking up residence with civilians, firing on an American force, and then exiting back up into the mountains. I was on a dirt trail walking between the huts when I stepped on a booby trap that had been buried and tied to a gate. I moved away quickly after it didn't go off.

Since I was only a couple of steps from Lt. Radcliffe when we moved on patrol, he began quizzing me almost every time we stopped with questions like, "Warden, where are we on the map?" or "What would you do now if we were hit, and you were in charge?" or "How would you call in artillery to the enemy if they were by that tree to our front?" I don't know why he gave me extra instruction or what he saw in me. I'd like to think he didn't accept me for what he saw. He just started treating me as if I were important. He started training me for leadership. The extra instruction he gave made me think about our surroundings and constantly think about planning for the unexpected event.

Radcliffe was a great map-reader. He had gone through Ranger school, the army's nine-week course on small unit tactics at Ft. Benning, GA. He would talk to me at length about how to do land navigation when we were moving at night or in triple-canopy forests. He would drill me on how to call in artillery fire missions and make me think about what kind of shells to ask for. I watched him call in several fire missions while I was his RTO, and I paid attention to what he did. One of the most important things he kept stressing was the use of pacing, especially at night. He made it sound so important that I procured a leather boot strap and when we were on the march at night or in heavy jungle, I would tie a knot for every hundred meters or steps that I walked. I really learned a lot from him. He seemed to want to have me ready for any situation. There's nothing more disconcerting to a group of soldiers than to have their leader be indecisive in times that called for a decision. I thought at the time, he was wasting his time on me. I was just a PFC with no authority over anyone. But, I think he saw more in me than I did.

In July 1967, our battalion traveled by C-130 aircraft to Kontum in the Central Highlands. Intelligence had reported that some of the Special Forces camps were reporting increased activity to their west. Our company camped next to an ARVN brigade just north of town. While there, Staff Sgt. Sablin returned to field after recovering from his wounds on May 31st at An Qui 1. He and another staff sergeant named Salas went around harassing all the lower rank enlisted guys.

He told me, "When I get you back in the 1st squad, I'm going to straighten you out!" I was glad I was an RTO for Lt. Radcliffe. He couldn't touch me as long as Radcliffe was around.

Lieutenant Radcliffe took a helicopter ride to scout the area around the Polei Kleng Special Forces Camp, which was west of Kontum. He returned in the afternoon and we began our trip west by truck on the highway, a dirt road devoid of bridges or any improvements at all. Along with our convoy were engineers who pulled a small bulldozer on a trailer behind their deuce and a half truck. The heavens opened up and we were soaked in the back of the uncovered trucks. It was pitch black dark along the way, and every few miles we encountered streams that were impassable. The engineers would unload the bulldozer in the dark. We would provide security, and they would move enough dirt to allow our convoy to continue on our way.

We arrived at Polei Kleng Special Forces camp the next morning. Outside the camp was a Montagnard village. These people were what the French dubbed "mountain people," hence the name Montagnards. We camped there a couple of days and then backpacked out, heading for the mountains. We were operating jointly with a group of Montagnards, armed and led by two Special Forces non-commissioned officers.

While we were with the Montagnards, we were introduced to Korean LRP rations. I don't know where they got them, but they traded some of these rations with us. The rations had some kind of red and black pepper that gave me gas like nobody's business.

A couple of days out, we were up in the foothills of a mountain range when the weather turned wet and cold. It probably got down to below sixty degrees Fahrenheit, and we were freezing. I took my turn at guard duty in a foxhole on our perimeter and watched the sun come up. Metz and Fletcher were asleep in a poncho hut behind the foxhole and since I had been feasting on the Korean LRP rations, I had a tremendous amount of gas. The thought came to mind that it would be funny to crawl back into the poncho hut, fart loudly, and tell Metz and Fletcher it was reveille.

I crawled back into the hooch and passed more gas than I had ever done in my life. The only problem was that gas was not all I passed. I had diarrhea so bad that it went all the way to the top of my boots and I was lying down.

Metz woke up and asked, "What in the world was that?"

To which I replied, "I've messed in my pants!"

Well, they kicked me out of the hooch and there I was in a real mess in more ways than one. I had just soiled the only pair of pants I had, and we still were going to be out more than a week or two. I walked down to a stream at the base of the hill, waded out into the freezing water and took my pants off and began to wash them as best I could. I looked around to see if anyone was watching, and to my chagrin about five Montagnards were taking their pants off and wading out to wash them, too. Montagnards thought American soldiers were cool and would imitate anything we did. I then hung my pants up, started a fire and promptly scorched my pants by putting them too close to the fire. I had to wear them another two weeks. I never tried to imitate a bugle call again.

FLYING HOWITZER

We air assaulted our company back up into the mountains around the last of June. The hill the helicopters set us on was covered with foliage about six to ten feet tall. We broke out the machetes, and by nightfall, we had cleared most of the hill and established a perimeter. Our captain had us dig three-man foxholes. The four platoons manned the perimeter and waited for nightfall.

About nine p.m., I sensed a strong smell of *nuoc mam*. Nuoc mam is fermented fish sauce made from storing large vats of small fish in containers for a considerable amount of time outside in hot weather. The sardines are then separated from the liquid, and what is left is the sauce. The Vietnamese eat the sauce on everything, especially rice, and it has a particularly strong odor that stays with the diner for quite some time. To me, it meant we had enemy soldiers very close to the perimeter. Word spread along the perimeter—along with the stench—that enemy soldiers were close. We lobbed grenades out into the brush, which was about twenty-five to thirty meters in front of us. We heard some screams and got a couple of rounds of return fire from AK-47s, but Radcliffe had warned us not to fire our weapons. Any flash from an M-16 or M-60 machine gun at night would have pinpointed where our foxholes were, and we didn't want that to happen.

The next day, we air assaulted via helicopter to another hill some officer picked out, called LZ Arbuckle. That officer must have been from Oklahoma, because the Arbuckle Mountains are in Southern Oklahoma. We went to work clearing the hill and cutting down the brush. We dug foxholes all around the hill that were big enough for three men. It was while we were clearing the brush in front of our foxholes that one of the guys was stuck with a nickname he would hate for the rest of his time in Vietnam.

As we cleared the brush, we piled it together for burning. We had gas cans with JP-4 (jet fuel) to start the fires. Cusick and I were sitting on the sandbags in front of his foxhole taking a break when one of the new guys, PFC Dennis Rasmussen of Minnesota, picked up a full can of fuel. He headed toward a pile of green brush that was smoldering. Both Cusick and I called out to him to watch about putting fuel on the brush pile.

He retorted back, "I've started a few fires in my time. You guys mind your own business!" He raised the can and began pouring the fuel on the pile. We watched the flame run up to the spout and into the can, causing it to explode and spray Rasmussen's face, arms, and hands. He took off running like a jackrabbit. Several guys caught him and rolled him over in the dirt to put out the flames. Rasmussen was a towhead and looked almost like an albino anyway. He looked terrible after being burned. He had to be medevaced immediately. That day he was dubbed "Torch" by the platoon. Despite his gross mistake that day, he eventually became a machine gunner, a really good soldier, and one of our inner circle of friends.

My foxhole was on the south side of the Arbuckle about fifty feet from where they were storing the artillery rounds and shells. On July 3rd, a CH-54 "Flying Crane" transport helicopter began bringing in four 155 mm howitzers to join the six 105 mm guns we already had on the top of the hill. As the CH-54 came in with the 155s suspended below, it generated a significant wind current. I had already experienced this wind when the 105s were delivered. Sand and dirt got in your hair and eyes. I had been picking big clots of dirt out of my hair for several days. Every time the helicopter delivered a gun, I covered up with my poncho to escape the wind and dirt.

On this particular pass, I covered up with a poncho as the Flying Crane came directly over my foxhole. I heard a loud "thump" behind me. I uncovered to look up hill and saw a 155 mm howitzer rolling down the hill. I sprang out of my hole and ran as hard as I could. I saw the 155 roll into my foxhole. I watched in horror as the gun pulled the CH-54 directly down to the ground. Helicopter blades began flying everywhere. One of the blades flew off and hit one of our guys in the 2nd platoon on top of the hill, slicing him in the stomach and exposing his intestines. The crew chief was out of the chopper even before it stopped, but the two pilots were trapped inside. I ran forward and got to the cockpit just as the fuselage stopped sliding down the hill. Lieutenant Radcliffe and I pulled the two pilots out and dragged them away from the wreckage. The whole mess had stopped right on top of my foxhole! Now it began to spark and burn. I had never seen a fire that burned from magnesium before, and this fire was burning white-hot. A shout went out that burning fragments had landed in the artillery dump. A couple of us went over and began moving the powder away from the flames of the burning pieces. Nobody was killed. The only person injured was our guy back up on the hill.

I went back up the hill to check on the injured guy and ran into the 2nd platoon leader, 1st Lt. Ralph Hagler. He looked me up and down and wisecracked, "Warden, are you as good as Radcliffe says?" I didn't know how to reply to that, since I didn't know what Radcliffe had said to the other platoon leaders, so I just smiled.

We did one patrol off Arbuckle. Led by Lt. Radcliffe, half of our platoon with one machine gun started down the southeast side of the mountain. We had been out about two hours when we took a break. Our point man came back to Radcliffe and whispered that he heard voices in front of him. The point man and Radcliffe went about one hundred meters to our front and observed a waterfall that poured into a pool. In the pool taking a bath were seven or eight enemy soldiers. Their weapons were stacked against a large rock bank on the side of the pool. Radcliffe came back for us, and we moved as quietly as we could down to get a clear view of the waterfall. One of our machine gunners took the safety off his weapon, aimed carefully and pulled the trigger. His M-60 fired one round and then quit firing. A couple of the guys nearest to him shot off a couple of rounds. The enemy soldiers beat a hasty retreat. All we found were tracks and some blood trails. The gunner checked his machine gun and found out he had loaded the gas cylinder backwards the last time he cleaned it.

On July 12, 1967, I was promoted to the rank of specialist 4th class. I think base pay for my new rank was around
$148 per month. It was the highest rank I ever expected or
hoped for, for the duration of my stint in the army. Only an
outstanding private or private 1st class who had joined the
army for a three-year hitch could expect to make sergeant
before his tour ended. Very few draftees could hope to see
E-5 during their short two-year career.

FIRST AWARD CEREMONY

We returned to the LZ English area and found ourselves ordered to the An Loa Valley, one of the most dreaded places to go in II Corps. It was a known fact that in times past, most of the population located there was in sympathy with the VC and NVA. There was a considerable amount of evidence that they gave them aid and sanctuary. Ambushes were a common occurrence for American forces. An Loa was in the Bong Son Area of Operations.

In April and May of 1967, the 227th Aviation Battalion dropped leaflets to warn the local population to get out of the area. The message announced that the An Loa would become a "free fire zone." In other words, anyone left in the area after May would be considered a combatant and be fired on by American troops. Even though there had been a number of major firefights in the Valley, we encountered no one. This was the first time we ever worked with a dog unit. We had a dog handler and a German shepherd the entire time we were in the An Loa Valley. We had them to guard against ambushes. The 1st Cav had lost a lot of men in there due to ambushes.

It was in the An Loa Valley that I had one of the strangest experiences of the war. There was any number of times we would be taking care of business in the field when someone in the rear would come up with a morale boosting idea on our behalf. It didn't matter whether it made sense to us or not; we would be thrust into some strange situations. This day was one of them. The colonel announced to our company commander that they were going to fly some sports equipment to us so we could have a little recreation. Sure enough, about noon, helicopters came bearing hot food, bats, gloves, softballs, badminton nets and rackets, and other sports paraphernalia too numerous to mention.

We couldn't play softball because of the knee-high grass, so we decided to use the softball as a football. We chose up sides, and it was the white guys against the black guys. About half of our platoon surrounded us and looked outward to keep someone from slipping up close to us and firing on us. On the other team were some good-sized guys, like Aaron Foster from , Fresno, CA. Aaron was about 6' 2" tall and barrel-chested. His size and demeanor made him look menacing, but his voice was soft and tender. He was one the most gentle guys I've ever known. He didn't have to act mean, he looked like he could have went bear hunting with a small stick. Aaron had a brother named Mac Foster who was a professional fighter from Fresno, CA. Aaron couldn't wait to get back to the states to resume working for his brother as a trainer.

At first we played two hands below the waist touch football. Then it turned into one hand below the waist touch football, and finally it was full body contact. I remember throwing a pass to a guy who caught it and then disappeared from sight as he ran out of the playing field and fell about ten feet into a creek. We literally beat each other to a pulp as the day wore on. In all of this, there was no racism or bigotry. The teams just came out like that.

About four p.m., a call came over my radio that we were to air assault to another location. We were told to bury the sports equipment and get ready to be picked up. There was no time for the helicopters to pick up the sports gear.

We were air assaulted further north, not too far from Highway 1, and were directed to the beach to cordon off a portion of it. In about thirty minutes, another helicopter landed with one lone individual on it. He was dressed in a wetsuit and had diving gear. Intelligence had told our battalion commander of NVA activity near this beach. They sent one Navy SEAL diver to check it out, and we were to watch his back. He went into the surf and was gone about twenty minutes. He came up from the surf dragging a body. He deposited his cargo on the beach and returned into the surf. This time he was gone about thirty minutes. He again came out of the surf with a body and placed it beside the other one. He had killed two NVA frogmen in hand-to-hand combat by himself. He then took off his oxygen tank, sat down beside the bodies, took out a cigarette, and lit it. It was one of the coolest scenes I have ever witnessed. We took a vote and deeded the beach to him. That Navy SEAL was one tough hombre.

Right after that episode, we were in the field north of Bong Son, when Rick Boeshart, Charlie Waskey, and I were ordered back to the rear on the morning chopper. We had no idea why we were being summoned to the rear, but we didn't care. At least we would be out of the field for a while. When we arrived at LZ English, the sergeant in charge of the rear area told us to go downtown, get a haircut, and take some new fatigues with us so we could have our name tags and patches sewn on. We were each being awarded the Silver Star medal for the action on May 31st–June 1st in an afternoon ceremony.

We caught a ride outside the gate to a barbershop, which was next to a bar and a house of prostitution. We proceeded to have a few cold beers while we got haircuts. We turned our fatigues in to the tailor to have our nametags, Cav patches and Combat Infantry Badges sewn on them. By the time we were through with the haircuts, shaves and new clothes, we were three sheets to the wind. The time for the awards ceremony was approaching, so we hitched a ride with a deuce and a half trucker going back to LZ English. Waskey and I climbed aboard in the back of the truck and hoisted Bo up with us. Bo stopped to take another swig of beer. The truck driver took off like a bat out of hell and Bo tumbled out the back. I ran forward to the cab of the truck and beat on it to have the driver stop. We backed up to Bo who was lying in the middle of the dirt road leading back to English. He had cuts and bruises everywhere, but he hadn't felt a thing. When we got back to the rear area, we cleaned Bo up as best we could and went to find the colonel. Col. Riddlehoover was all decked out in clean, starched fatigues. When he came in front of me, I was at least halfway presentable, but when he stepped in front of Bo to have the citation read aloud, he was obviously displeased. Bo was rocking back and forth so much that the colonel had to grab hold of his lapel to keep him from falling over backwards. We got through the ceremony without any reprimand, so I guess we did all right. We had to go back out on the chow chopper that evening. So much for medals and ceremonies, but it got us out of the field for awhile. I collected my Silver Star, a Bronze Star for Valor and a Purple Heart and left them at the rear area to be mailed to my mother.

We went on a cordon mission one night in company strength. We were in the Bong Son Plain somewhere. It was pitch black dark. We were trying to be very quiet and surround a village in the dark. Early in the morning, the Vietnamese National Police would be called in to interrogate the villagers. We came upon a bridge that had all the wooden planks gone from it. That left just the two extensions of angle iron going over the river. We were instructed in whispers to get down on our butts, straddle the angle iron, and use our arms to push ourselves across the bridge. Lt. Radcliffe and I made it across with the 3rd platoon and then the 2nd platoon began their trip across the bridge. A guy in 2nd platoon named Dennis Horin lost his balance and fell off the bridge. He screamed all the way down until he hit the water. Then he called out to tell everyone that he had lost his M-16. I remember the CO (commanding officer) was going to make him pay the $136 that M-16s cost the army.

We called Horin "The Mouth" because he was always talking. One day, we were notified that Secretary of the Army Stanley Resor was going to be paying us a visit. They sent Horin and another guy up to meet the helicopter bringing Resor and his entourage. He and the other guy were to come to attention with their M-16s at parade rest. When the helicopter landed, Horin immediately stuck out his hand and introduced himself to Resor. He told him where he was from and started a conversation about some topic he had on his mind. Resor had a hard time getting away from him. Even the guys who have difficulty remembering names, places, and faces remember the guy who fell off the bridge and screamed all the way down that night.

Another night in July, a soldier on guard duty on LZ English took a parachute flare and fired it in front of his perimeter because he thought he saw movement. It sailed backwards toward the doorway of an underground bunker where artillery rounds and ammo were stored. It caused a gigantic explosion and fireworks display. We watched the explosions for hours from our position up in the mountains around the Bong Son Plain. I heard they never found out who the guy was who was responsible for firing the flare. We considered this our own private Fourth of July fireworks display. It was an amazing display of color.

The Bong Son Plain was the coastal area between the Central Highlands and the coast of the South China Sea, north of Bong Son city and the Bong Son River. It was flat and composed mostly of rice paddies that covered an area of about two to three miles in width and about ten to fifteen miles in length. Looking somewhat like small islands, there would be dry land in the middle of these rice paddies with one or several houses. When we did night movement on the Plain, we would hike over the rice paddy dikes to this dry land and form a perimeter looking out toward the rice paddies.

It was on one such night that something hilarious happened. Our entire platoon was around an uninhabited house that sat on one of these islands in the middle of huge rice paddies. We were bedded down for the night under palm trees and a full moon. Only about 10 percent of our guys were on guard duty.

About two or three o'clock in the morning, Rick Boeshart shook me awake, saying very angrily, "Doug, did you hit me in the face?" I was taken aback by Rick's display of anger. Bo was the most even tempered guy I have ever met. I looked at his face in the full moonlight and saw that he had a huge swelling just under one eye. He looked like he had taken a beating in a fistfight. After I told him I had not hit him, he went to everybody who was sleeping around him and asked the same question. He was becoming even more upset with each question. We finally assured him that no one had hit him while he was asleep and got him to go back to bed after he saw the medic. The next morning we found what had happened. He was sleeping on his back and a coconut had fallen from one of the trees and hit him square in the face. We all got a big laugh out of the situation at his expense.

FILLING TIME

Now began a series of monotonous days that lasted through July. We would stay out two or three weeks at a time and then come back into LZ English for a stand down. When we came back into English, we usually stayed one night. We would come in usually in the middle of the afternoon to showers and a hot meal. Then we would go downtown in groups of two or three. The rule was that we had to wear our steel pots (helmets) and carry M-16s with one magazine. We could get a haircut and neck massage at the barbershop. I would have bet the local barber was connected to the local VC cells. Some of the guys let the barber do a disgusting ear cleaning. I never wanted to have that done. I'm not going to describe what was done, but you can use your imagination.

Before dark, we were to be back inside the compound at English. There was an Enlisted Men's Club there, as well as an Officer's Club. The EM Club would usually stay open until about eight p.m. at night. If it were closed, we would go to the chaplain's tent and buy beer from him. Some nights, in a drunken stupor, we would steal beer from him, but looking back on it, I'm sure he heard us and just let us help ourselves.

I found an old, cheap, six-string guitar with a plywood top in our tent in the rear. I would lead the guys in song as we drank beer. I could sing a version of the Shadows of the Night's "Gloria." Then I would start in on a series of songs I knew by heart. I would sing Roger Miller's "King of the Road" and Charlie Pride's "Green Green Grass of Home." It was usually the guys I was closest to who would all congregate around and either sing along or listen. Tom Cusick, David Wilkowski, Rick Boeshart, Calvin Gouley, Charlie Waskey, Duane McAndrews, and Alvin Nibbelink, would all be drinking Carling Black Label or Hamm's beer.

My singing ability always got better as I drank more and more. In reality, I couldn't carry a tune in a bucket. I would sing songs like "Gloria" and a song I made up to the tune of "Movin' On." I don't remember all of it, but one verse began, "Hear the pitter patter of rumbling feet, it's the 1st Cav Division in full retreat." One night Rick Boeshart listened to me sing the "Green, Green Grass of Home," and as I finished the last refrain, he said, "Damn, Doug, that sure was pretty." He shed a tear and took another drink. We did anything to drink to the point that we could ease the pain we felt in our chest. It was a combination of homesickness, stress, and fear of dying that ate at us all the time. We were all about nineteen to twenty-two years of age and didn't know how to handle the events that were happening around us. It wasn't too long until the six-string guitar became a five-string guitar, and finally it was a four-string guitar. We didn't care; it was something to do.

We watched movies when we were in the rear. We frequently watched episodes of *Combat* with Vic Morrow. It was a black and white series that was on TV back in the States. I guess the recreation people in the rear got a new installment every week or so. We never took it serious. We would get a good laugh at the tactics they used and the battle scenes. It was not even close to the real thing. The sound of gunfire in the movies is always recorded as outgoing fire. It's only when you hear the "spat" or 'plump" of an incoming round that it is close to realistic.

It wasn't until "Saving Private Ryan" and "We Were Soldiers Once" that I thought a movie captured war realistically. The difference in these movies is that the sound of the gunfire is filmed from a different perspective. It is recorded as if the gun is aimed at the camera. There is a distinct difference between the sound of outgoing and incoming rounds. These movies captured that sound, and it was eerie.

My mom faithfully wrote to me often. Once a week, she would fold the hometown newspaper, the Prague Record, and put it in with her letters in a large envelope. Whenever the guys spotted the large envelope handed out to me at mail call, they would gather round. They all wanted to see what the news was in a small town in Oklahoma. We all got a big kick out of an article about a bobcat being killed on someone's front porch. The article was accompanied by a photograph of the dead bobcat on display. The guys thought it was really funny to see that kind of story on the front page. I could never hide any piece of mail that arrived for me. The guys watched out for me to get a letter or goodies from home.

One day, I went outside the perimeter to dig a "cat hole" to take a dump. While I was squatting down, a sniper opened up on me, and I really had to scramble to get behind something to give me cover. I hadn't taken my M-16 rifle with me, and I was very uncomfortable being in that position without a weapon. I wrote to my mom and dad and asked them to find me a pistol back home to send to me. I told them to mail it to me with "FILM, DO NOT X-RAY" on the outside of the box. The guys in my platoon told me it would make it through without being inspected. So I waited, and in about three weeks, here came a package for me with the words, "FILM, DO NOT X-RAY" on the outside. I opened it up and there was a .38 caliber Smith & Wesson snub-nosed pistol with a scabbard. There was also a package of film for my Kodak Instamatic. Mom just couldn't tell a lie. If the box said it contained a roll of film, she would make sure that it was so. I've always admired and respected her for her honesty and integrity.

My Aunt Betty (my mom's sister) had a friend who had been with the US Postal Service for quite some time. He was also a WWII veteran. So, whenever Betty would send me candy or some kind of perishable, Jimmy McFarland would put the items in an aluminum container and seal it with rivets. I would sometimes spend hours getting the package open, but the contents were always intact!

There was no way to hide anything from anyone in our platoon. Everybody knew pretty much everything about everybody else. From chowtime to dark, the time when we usually moved to a new position, there was plenty of time to read letters, share goodies from home, gossip, complain, tell about your girlfriends, wives, parents, brothers, sisters, etc. I told some of my friends back then some of the most intimate details of my life. It's hard to describe how close we were. Even though there were some of the guys I didn't feel that close to, I knew who the ones were that I could count on when the bullets were flying.

It was during this time that I became acquainted with Staff Sgt. Fanning. He was an anomaly in our company. He had been in Vietnam since the early 1960s with Special Forces. According to him, he was kicked out of Special Forces and came to Charlie Company in 1966. He was in the 2nd platoon. He was married to a Vietnamese woman. I don't know where she lived, but he would take an occasional R&R and go to be with her. He didn't ever want to go back to the States. I had a hard time understanding what he was all about.

One night we were on the march in the Bong Son Plain in company strength after a heavy rain. Ahead of us, we heard a terrifying sound. We didn't know what the sound was at first. Up front from our column was a deep hole that used to have a roof on it. It was a blown bunker. The hole was filled with a couple feet of water. In it was a water buffalo. He was tethered with a rope attached to his nose ring. When he smelled us, he began to sound a warning through his nose. His fear caused him to pull loose from his rope, pull the ring from his nose, and charge straight for our point man. We all jumped to the side of the trail into several inches of mud. We watched this huge, black thing charge right through us on a moonless night. A few of the guys fired their M-16s at him, but it didn't faze him. It scared us half to death. It took several minutes to find everybody in the dark to resume our march.

At some point in July when we were camped somewhere in the daytime, a few of us borrowed pistols, unloaded them, and had quick draw contests with each other. I was about as fast as anybody, and it was great fun to try to outdraw each other. One day Fletcher borrowed a .45 caliber pistol to go down in a hole. When he came out of the hole, he returned the pistol half cocked to the guy who had loaned it to him. I think his name was Jetco or Jetmore, and he was from California. The gun went off and he shot himself in the side of his leg. The wound started at his hip and went all the way to his knee. He was medevaced, and we never saw him again. Several of the guys had to go back to the rear later to write sworn statements about the event. The guy who had shot himself was in court-martial proceedings back in the States.

There are some strange thoughts that go through your mind in combat. I couldn't remember what the dashboard looked like on my mom and dad's 1957 Chevrolet. I would spend hours during guard at night or while on the march trying to remember what it looked like. I also dreamed of cheeseburgers and a cold glass of milk. I got to the point that I would have spent a month's pay on just one cheeseburger and a cold glass of milk. I didn't fantasize about girls, just food and cars while in the field.

We all met Charlton Heston at LZ Geronimo, just north of LZ English. I was lying on my back, taking a nap inside the sandbagged bunkers early one morning. Someone came into our bunker, and we all rose up to see who it was. Someone reached down to me and shook my hand. I looked up to the man who had played "Moses." He left just as quickly as he had entered. I looked at the other guys in the bunker and asked, "Was that Charlton Heston?" They thought it was him also.

It was on Geronimo that I first saw a starlight scope. It was a device that allowed someone to see shapes in the dark. Even on a moonless night, when it was turned on, you could see shapes such as trees, bushes, and houses in the dark. It was pretty fuzzy—it looked like it was snowing in the scope. The background was green, and the shapes showed up as white. There was some guy from the rear that brought it out, and it was not supposed to leave his possession.

We used the starlight scope one night as we pulled a patrol off of Geronimo. The guy from the rear who was responsible for it would not go with us on night patrol, even though we invited him. Charles Fletcher was point man, and he used the starlight scope to help us find our way as we followed the path through the concertina wire and then moved east downhill to the floor of the Bong Son Plain. Fletcher got to the bottom of the hill and raised the scope to look around. As he swung the scope up to his eye, he realized he was looking at a face looking at him from behind a tree about six feet from him. He dropped the scope and opened up on full automatic. He completely missed the VC and the VC ran off into the night. We took about five minutes to find the starlight scope on the ground and then resumed our patrol. Fletch, as we called Fletcher, was a black guy from Oklahoma City. He had a great physique, and was always showing off his "six pack" stomach in the pictures that we took of him. He loved a good joke or story and had an infectious laugh that made you want to laugh with him. Since he was short in stature, he became one of our tunnel rats. I thought at the time that I was glad that I was tall, since it excluded me from going down into holes with a .45 caliber pistol and a flashlight. But, Fletch was good at it and never tried to get out of going down into the holes to look for the enemy. I admired him tremendously for his courage.

On one of our patrols from Geronimo during the day, I witnessed an event that was really bizarre. We came to a house that had a locked door. One of our guys moved to an open window and threw in a grenade. He then backed up against the wall to let the grenade go off. What he forgot was that the wall was made of grass. Some of the fragments hit him in the back and blew him away from the house. He wasn't seriously injured, but he had to be medevaced.

Another event I remember on Geronimo was watching a movie in the mess hall tent—"*The Fastest Guitar in the West.*" Perhaps the worst movie I have ever seen, it starred the singer Roy Orbison as Johnny Banner, a confederate spy traveling undercover as a guitar instructor. Johnny Banner had a pistol in his guitar to shoot his foes. I've heard and read since then that even Elvis Presley wouldn't consider doing this movie. During the viewing, a mortar attack on our position caused us to scramble for the bunkers. They didn't try to show it again. I was glad.

While I'm on the subject of LZ Geronimo, I must say something about the unit for which we were usually pulling security on Geronimo. It was B Battery, 2nd Battalion (Airborne), 19th Artillery, the same bunch that had been with Charlie Company on LZ Bird in December 1966 when twenty-nine artillerymen and infantrymen were killed. There was a closeness and trust between Charlie Company and B Battery. When in the field, we were able to get first round HE from B Battery. That's how much confidence they had in our capabilities and we in their ability. Usually, when artillery is called in, the first round is a smoke round. From where the smoke round lands, adjustments are made and then HE rounds are fired. B Battery always had four people with us as forward observers. It was usually a lieutenant and a recon sergeant or recon corporal with two guys who carried their radios. All of the people we had from B Battery were top-notch soldiers.

One of my good friends caught the clap from one of his escapades to a whorehouse in downtown Bong Son. It got so bad that when I looked back at him when we were on patrol, I saw a big wet spot around his groin area. He was married and had less than a month to go before he would go back to the States. Lt. Radcliffe kept him out in the field to teach him a lesson about staying clean before going back to the States. He had a lot of pain every time he tried to urinate. Radcliffe finally relented and sent the guy back and told him to stay away from downtown until he went home. The guy pulled KP every day until it was his time to go home.

Lt. Radcliffe was just about to complete his six months in the field. Officers would spend six months in the field and then spend six months in the rear, doing some staff job. He had spent January through March 1967 in the field, then he had been in the rear as the XO March through May, and now he was slated to become the XO again. Without consulting me, he talked with our new company commander,

Capt. Patti, about my coming to the company command post to become the chief RTO. He told me later it was his way of giving me a better chance of making it through my tour of duty. So in mid August, I became the chief RTO for the company commander. I thought I would like him, since he was a service academy graduate like Bob Radcliffe, but it was not to be.

PART IV:
SQUAD LEADER

COMPANY COMMO CHIEF

I was now assigned to the company CP, which consists of the company commander, an RTO to carry the company radio, an RTO to carry the battalion radio, an RTO to carry a radio that linked us to the S-3 air officer who arranged for our helicopter lifts and support, an RTO to carry the artillery radio and the head medic for the company.

Capt. Patti was the company commander. He was an Air Force Academy graduate who had chosen to take an Army commission. He was also an airborne ranger and was about to make major. I carried the battalion radio, Whitmore carried the S-3 air radio, Harold Bauer carried the company radio, Buehler carried the artillery radio and Joe "Doc" O'Keefe was the head medic. My call sign was Smoking Barrel Six India and my main contact to battalion was Cold Pistol 65. He was the liaison to the battalion commander. We had to call in a situation report to Cold Pistol 65 at the top of every hour, twenty-four hours a day, no matter where we were. This information went into a daily staff journal for the battalion. It told where each company was located, what its situation was and how many patrols and listing posts it had out at any given time.

Buehler made a habit of going to sleep on radio watch. For two nights in a row, there was no one calling in situation reports back to battalion, and the colonel gave Capt. Patti fits about it. Patti questioned each one of us about our involvement in the incidents, but he couldn't see that Buehler was the problem. So he told me that since I was in charge, he was giving me an Article 15 and fining me one month's pay for the incident.

I was really steamed about this. I told him I knew who was responsible, and if he couldn't figure it out, then he could take the money and I would make sure it didn't happen again. I started putting Buehler on the first and last watch, but it wasn't fair to the rest of the guys and I thought it was very poor leadership on the captain's part to handle it that way. When the order to give me an Article 15 got back to the rear, Lt. Radcliffe squelched it, and I never lost any money, and there was never an Article 15 that made it to my personnel file. Radcliffe thought it was unfair also.

I learned how inept Capt. Patti was when we were walking in the Bong Son Plain around August 19th or 20th, and we began drawing sniper fire. I looked to our left and could see the outline of a Viet Cong lying prone shooting at our left flank. I fired two or three rounds in his direction and Capt. Patti went to a prone shooting position and began firing in that general direction. He was firing in the right direction, but in a prone position, he was shooting directly at our left flank guys. I was shooting about four or five feet over their heads, while his rounds were spraying all around them. They weren't sure which direction the rounds were coming from with Capt. Patti firing on full automatic.

"What the heck are you doing?" I screamed at Patti. He just stared back at me blankly. Eventually he stood up and continued on.

That very day the sniper wounded one of our sergeants in the chest. His name was Norman Dale. He lay around twenty-five meters to our front when the sniper fire increased. Staff Sgt. Felix Salas, a native of Guam and friend of Staff Sgt. Sablin, yelled out, "I'll go get him if someone will put me in for a medal!" He crawled out on his stomach to get Sgt. Dale. His actions were great, but the minute he got back inside our perimeter he started asking for someone to write him up for a medal. I had never imagined anyone doing that. I thought good manners dictate that two members of our unit would get together and write him up for a citation. He did get a medal for that action, though I'm not sure what he received. Personally, I thought the whole thing was a joke. How could he have any self-respect? And who cared about medals, anyway? For lifers, certain medals were linked to point systems used for promotions. I guess he had his eye on making E-7. .

SSG Salas was one of the most disliked guys in our platoon. When he first arrived and took over a squad, he threw a poncho rain coat at Dennis Rasmussen and told him to build him a tent for the night. Rasmussen threw it back to him and said, "Make your own tent, I'm not your servant!" After some other friction between these two, Rasmussen told Salas that he better not ever get in front of him in a firefight. I don't think that Rasmussen really meant it, though. In October, 1967, Salas was wounded by a booby trap. He screamed all the way to the medevac chopper that Rasmussen had shot him. Dennis took a lot of pride in being blamed by Salas for his wounds.

We were someplace in the jungle, crossing a log bridge over a creek in the rain. I followed Capt. Patti across the log. It was about ten feet to the other side. I got about half-way across when I slipped and fell onto the bridge on my tailbone. Then, I slowly slipped off the log and fell another ten feet to the bottom of the creek. I lay there a long time before I tried to get up. My back was killing me and as we again started to move out, my back began to hurt more and more.

That evening I got on the chow chopper after it delivered our meal and went back to the rear to the doctor. They took some x-rays and had me moved to the 85th Evac Hospital in Qui Nhon. I was there for about a week in and out of traction. I was in a bed between two guys—an Army engineer who had swung an oversized hammer and messed up the blood vessels in his right arm and another guy who had been circumcised because he had picked up an infection. When I could walk around, some of us would hang pictures of Playboy centerfolds around his bed. We thought it was funny; he didn't.

I ran into Staff Sgt. Merritt, a sergeant from the weapons platoon. He had white hair all over his body. I remember I didn't trust him. He was a decent enough guy, but he was a lifer and I didn't want much to do with him. About the time I was discharged from the hospital, Sgt. Merritt and I were walking past a lieutenant colonel and his aide, a captain. I didn't salute but Merritt did. The captain called me back and made me salute him. He asked why I didn't salute a superior officer. I told him I came from the field where we didn't salute. A salute in the field would allow any VC that was watching to identify who the officers were and shoot at them. I got off with a lecture, but it fell on deaf ears.

I was able to go down to the USO Club for a hamburger. It was the first hamburger I had tasted in about six months. There was a guy playing the piano in the corner of the main room. He was very talented and took requests from the guys sitting around listening to him.

My stay was finally over, and I caught a ride to the airfield and put my name on a list to go back to An Khe. After I got to An Khe, I caught a helicopter going back to Bong Son.

BOY SERGEANT

After I came back from the 85th Evac Hospital around the second week of September, I promptly announced to Capt. Patti that I could not carry a radio with a sore back. He sent me back to the 3rd platoon. I guess anybody else would have stayed where I was, but I was fed up with Buehler. I was sent to the CP because I had done a good job, but I didn't fit in very well with others who didn't do their job. I don't want you to think Bauer and Whitmore were slackers; they were good soldiers. It was Buehler I had the problem with.

I remember going to the platoon leader, and he assigned me to the first squad. Since I outranked the current squad leader who had been in country since last February, I was the new squad leader. I had six guys and me. They were Phillip Hayes and David Wilkowski, both M-79 grenadiers; and Buster Morgan, Luis Arroyo, Alvin Nibbelink, and Calvin Gouley, all riflemen.

"Tyke" Hayes was from my home state and grew up on a farm near Chelsea, OK. He was about six feet tall, had brown hair, and was the epitome of a country boy. His favorite pastime back home was coon hunting. He had raised champion bluetick hounds for coon hunting. As a matter of fact, after he got back to the farm, his hounds were used in the Disney film, "*Where the Red Fern Grows.*" He always had a smile on his face that made him look like Huckleberry Hound, a cartoon character. We were not the first to notice his likeness to cartoon dogs because he told all of us to call him "Tyke."

Dave Wilkowski was the best shot with an M-79 grenade launcher I had ever seen. On two occasions I saw him hit a running enemy soldier at over one hundred yards with an M-79 round. He was skinny as a rail, about five-foot-eleven and could carry more M-79 rounds than any grenadier in the company. He was from Saint Claire Shores near Detroit. Dave didn't say much, but when he did, it was always very profound and to the point. Willie "Buster" Morgan was from Groesbeck, Texas. He was a young, athletic-looking black kid, who rarely spoke a word. He always did his best to do everything I said and never refused an order. He was a great soldier. I got him promoted to buck sergeant right after the Tet Offensive. When I left the field, I recommended him to take my squad, though he didn't. Buster didn't want the leadership role. At times, he had trouble with his emotions dealing with fear. I'm afraid that it consumed him after I left the field.

Luis Arroyo, Kansas City, had already been in country for over a year. He had fairly long, black hair and was about five-foot-eight. He had been a guard at Long Bihn Jail, affectionately called, "LBJ." He loved to smoke marijuana, and since he loved it so much and it was so abundant, he extended as an infantryman to stay in country to smoke it. He was the one weak link I had to manage.

Alvin Nibbelink only had a couple of months left before he was to go home to Iowa. He was the squad leader before I came back, and I anticipated I would have trouble from him, though I never did. I think he was relieved to have someone take over for him. He also was pretty quiet and didn't say much, except to Wilkowski. They were pretty close buddies with Rick Boeshart, one of the machine gunners in our platoon. They had all came to the field together in February of 1967.

Calvin Gouley, who was from Detroit, Michigan, walked point for me more than anyone else. He even went so far as to order a shotgun with slugs in it so he could have a good weapon in the heavy jungle when he walked point. Gouley was sandy haired, was about five-foot-seven and a better soldier in the field than back in the rear. If we were back in the rear and you turned around, Gouley would be gone. He hated pulling any kind of detail back in the rear.

All in all, I thought I had a pretty good group. They were all experienced and knew what they were doing. All were draftees, with the exception of Arroyo who was Regular Army. Since I wasn't a sergeant, the guys wanted to know what to call me. I told them to call me by my first name, just as they had from the start of my tour. After I was promoted to the rank of sergeant, I made the rest of the sergeants in the company address me as Sgt. Warden, but I let all the guys call me Doug. It infuriated the lifers a lot, but I did it just to irritate them.

My promotion to sergeant E-5 came in September. The pay was $211 per month. We used to have a sign someone had stapled over the door in our barracks back in An Khe. It showed WWI soldiers marching through mud with the caption, "You, too, can see Southeast Asia on less than eight dollars a day." The pay was not much, but the experience was worth far more than the pay.

Looking back on the decision to make me a squad leader, I have often wondered if Bob Radcliffe had anything to do with their choice. He was, after all, still the XO of the company. I know he lobbied for me to become the chief RTO for the company commander. But I took the promotion as a sign that the officers were confident I could do the job. I had to make sure my squad was fed, clothed, took their malaria pills once a week, cleaned their weapons, and didn't walk around with their weapons without the safety in the off position. I had to choose the guy who walked point when it came our time to lead, pick guard duty rosters, and so on. Looking after details like those was not what made a leader, though. It wasn't long before I began experiencing a long series of tests to my leadership qualities.

In September 1967, we lost all the airborne enlisted personnel who were drawing jump pay below the rank of E-5. Only the NCOs, sergeant E-5 and above, were allowed to receive jump pay and were retained, so as not to deplete the ranks of experienced NCOs. The enlisted guys were transferred to other airborne units, such as the 82nd Airborne, the 101st Airborne and the 173rd Airborne.

We were in the Bong Son Plain on operations a couple of days later. I believe our company commander at that time was a Capt. McDonald. He was from Oklahoma and came from Headquarters Company. The 3rd platoon was picked to lead us to a village for a cordon mission that night. I went over the order I wanted the squad to walk in and even took Arroyo, whom I picked to walk point, on a recon of the trail that we were to take. We viewed the village from a distance, and I estimated how far we would walk. It was a relatively simple operation, or so I thought.

Nighttime has a way of confusing direction and distance. After many night operations, I learned that you almost always think you have walked the correct distance, when the truth is that you are just short of the objective. That night we saddled up and moved out with Arroyo in the lead, Wilkowski second, and I was third in the column. We hadn't gone very far when I realized Arroyo was high on pot. I pushed forward and stopped him.

I got close to him and whispered, "What's wrong? You are weaving all over the trail and you're going too slow."

He answered, "I've been smoking some joints and I'm having trouble seeing." I told him I would deal with him later.

Since I was the only one who had seen the objective, I put myself on point. We continued toward the village. We hadn't gone very far when my platoon leader sent word up to stop. He walked up to me and asked why we weren't at the objective yet I answered that I thought we were still about one thousand meters away. He stated that he didn't think so. He thought we had passed through the village about five hundred yards back. I argued that it was still ahead. I started to explain that I had been counting my paces, but he ordered me to start toward the rear of the company. This was the second time we had stopped on this pitch-black dark night. So as we were doubling back through the company column, I got several choice comments like, "Don't you know what you're doing, Warden?" and "Don't you know how to read a map?" I was beginning to boil. As we passed by the company commander, he stopped the platoon leader to ask, "What's the problem?"

The platoon leader started to explain that we had passed our objective, but the CO stopped him and looked at me.

He asked, "What do you think, Warden?"

I told him I thought we hadn't gone far enough. He told the lieutenant to turn around and continue.

The platoon leader whispered to me, "Warden, don't you ever make me look bad to the Old Man again."

We continued and finally came to the village. I was right about where it was located. As everybody filed past us to take up their positions around the village, I got several choice comments again, questioning my map reading ability. This was the first time, but not the last that my lieutenant and I disagreed over our location.

The next day, after the village had been searched thoroughly, I tore into Arroyo. I told him in no uncertain terms that he could smoke anything he wanted to when he was in the rear, but if he pulled a stunt like that again while we were in the field, he would be an inmate at LBJ.

A little later in the day, I was told to take a couple of my guys and scout on down the trail east. I took Gouley and Wilkowski with me. We had gone about eight hundred meters, when we started drawing small arms fire. Gouley and Wilkowski were up ahead of me when we hit the dirt. This was the time every leader dreads. They both looked back at me as if to say, "What do we do now?" I didn't do anything. I watched as Gouley and then Wilkowski got up and moved forward out of sight. I lay there for what seemed an eternity. Thoughts of fear were moving through my mind about being wounded and killed. Then a thought came into my mind that screamed at me, "How can you lead men way back here?" That caused me to get up and catch up with my guys.

We moved toward a cave off the trail, and Gouley threw in a concussion grenade. A fresh skeleton flew out of the cave—most of the flesh had been blown off the corpse by the concussion grenade. We continued to draw small arms fire, so I had Wilkowski stay where he was, and I indicated to Gouley that we should flank the guy who was shooting at us and try to stop him. We moved out and hadn't advanced very far when the rest of the company showed up. I pointed out to one of the platoon leaders the approximate position of the sniper and they moved out. Under my command, my squad claimed its first enemy kill that day. As I reflected about it later, I decided I had performed pretty well after my initial response to just lie there and stay behind my two guys. I had observed leadership before, but it was my first time to really lead when the bullets were flying. I decided from that day forward I would be in front of my guys, leading them into the action, rather than ordering them from behind.

TAKING CHARGE

Before the Vietnam presidential elections in September 1967, there was a real concern that the Viet Cong and the NVA would start terrorist attacks against the civilians who would be voting. I think Gen. Thieu and Vice Air Marshall Ky were on one ticket, though I don't remember who was running against them. We had been staying on LZ Lowboy during the day up until the elections. The week before they started, our company took two squads and assigned them to one APC (armored personnel carrier) per checkpoint along Highway 1. This would create an armed presence to protect the civilian voters who used the highway to get to the ballot locations.

On one particular day, we were parked near a bridge on Highway 1, just north of Lowboy. After dark, we would keep a couple of the men awake to guard the bridge against any sabotage. I was talking to my platoon leader just after dusk when a tremendous crashing sound came from about fifty meters west of the bridge. It sounded like an elephant had fallen down a fifteen-foot embankment. Rick Boeshart, our machine gunner, opened up on my command, and fired about three hundred rounds into the dark. Every sixth round was a tracer, so we could see exactly where he was firing. I climbed on top of the APC and opened up with the M-60 mounted on it. I fired until the barrel of the gun was glowing red in the dark. We stopped and listened. We didn't hear another sound.

I think we intercepted one of two things—either it was a VC Sapper group with explosives approaching us to blow up the bridge, or it was a livestock animal that lost its footing on a ridge near the bridge. One or the other fell down and made a lot of noise. I doubled the guard, but we heard nothing else during that night.

One very tragic event happened while we were on operations in Bong Son in October 1967. On the night of October 25th, we were moving in company formation, when our point man, Scott Smith, came up on two VC who were hunched down in the dark. Instead of halting, Smith charged both of them, firing his shotgun as he took them on in the dark. After they fled because of his aggressive charge, we found they had two US claymore mines that they were attempting to arm for an ambush on our column. Smith probably saved several lives with his charge. I believe someone had the presence of mind to put him in for a Bronze Star for Valor.

He was a close friend of Stan Tunall in the 1st platoon. Scotty and Stan were from the same area around Orange County, CA. They were both draftees and planned on getting out about the same time and rooming together while they attended college on the GI Bill.

The next day, Stan was sitting to Scotty's left while Scotty was cleaning his shotgun. We kept one shotgun for each platoon. It was handy for the point man to use, especially when we were in dense jungle. The shotguns were loaded with double aught buckshot. Scotty somehow put some pressure on the trigger of the shotgun that he thought was unloaded, and it hit Stan full force in the side of his face. We were all distraught, but Scotty was beside himself. They sent Scotty back to the rear to the doctor.

On October 27th, after the elections, we were air assaulted to the mountains. I recognized Hill 405 where I had spent my first night in the field. We moved in company formation quickly back toward the Bong Son Plain. We moved across a creek, and I recognized it as the creek where we had encountered the VC we had killed prior to the firefight on May 31st. Across the creek, there were three grave mounds where the VC had been buried. I guess their comrades had come back to find their bodies where we left them and they had buried them.

We continued on and broke out of the mountains. We were headed for a single mountain that rose from the sea and was perhaps four hundred to five hundred meters in circumference. At this point we received word that hamburgers, soft drinks and beer were going to be flown to us after we reached the beach by the mountain. On the way there, we walked along Highway 1 for a while. I noticed a deuce and a half truck driver go past, and I realized I knew him. I couldn't remember his name, but I was certain he was from my hometown. When he drove back by after dumping his load, I aimed my M-16 in the air and fired off a burst. He stopped his truck and headed for the ditch as fast as he could. I walked back and stood over him.

I said, "I don't remember your name, but I know you're from Prague!"

He was from Prague. His name was Mike Click, and he had been a sophomore when I was a senior at Prague High. We talked for a minute and I got the idea to ask him to accompany us. I notified my platoon leader that I would join them later. Mike drove back to his unit about a mile away, and we asked his commander if he could have lunch with us if I would guarantee his safe return. We walked back to the beach by the mountain. It was really great to see someone from home. It didn't matter that we had never been friends.

Our visit was cut short when we couldn't find two of our guys. Both Tom Naile from Missouri and Dave Baker, a black soldier, were last seen swimming and holding on to an air mattress they had blown up to use as a life preserver. The undertow from the ocean pulled them under, and they both drowned. After this tragic event, I walked Mike back up the road to the LZ where he was stationed and bid him farewell. It was the last time I saw him. Naile and Baker were found a couple of days later by a helicopter flying over the South China Sea. I was flown back to the rear to identify both bodies.

One night we were on LZ Geronimo pulling "palace guard," and I was in one of the bunkers. My platoon leader came down and asked me to come outside with him. He led me to the edge of the western side of our perimeter. He asked me to listen for a while. I heard several shrieks and then laughter. I asked him to explain what it was. He said he didn't know, but whatever it was, it was coming from my guys who were outside the perimeter pulling listening post. And they wouldn't answer their radio. He said, "They are your guys; you go get them and bring them in."

They were at least two hundred meters outside of the perimeter. So, here I go out in the pitch-black darkness to get three armed men who don't know I'm coming. I cautiously walked about a hundred meters and then got down on my stomach and crawled the remaining hundred meters. When I got out to my guys, I found out what was going on. Gouley and Hayes had brought a joint with them and had given a couple of drags to Buster Morgan. Morgan had never smoked pot before and began seeing snakes all around him. He had a mortal fear of snakes and screamed bloody murder. Gouley and Hayes thought it was hysterical and laughed like hyenas.

I got them in tow and brought them back inside the perimeter. I put them in a bunker to sleep it off. My platoon leader told me he was going to court-martial them. I told him that if I was to have any authority over them in the future, he should let me handle it. The next day I sent in the information for them all to get an Article 15 (forfeiture of pay). I fined them a month's pay but kept them from losing their rank. I got up close and personal with them and told them that if I ever had to come out to get them again while they were smoking dope, I would just empty my M-16 on them. I didn't really mean it, but I hoped they didn't know it. I never had any problems with them again.

There were a number of tricks I picked up from the old guys. I learned you could take a piece of fishing line or catgut and tie one end to a 5.56 mm round and the other to the end of your rifle, and it became a device for point men to use to alert them to booby traps. The line suspended from the rifle would bend when it came in contact with a trip wire for a booby trap. When you saw the line bend, you knew to back up and check things out.

Another trick I learned was to use a tracer round for the next to the last round in each magazine in my ammo pouches. There's nothing worse than having just one round in your chamber when you come in contact with the enemy. The tracer round kept that from happening.

I also learned to construct automatic ambushes. I unscrewed the pin from a regular grenade and replaced it with the firing pin from a smoke grenade. The pin on a regular grenade has a four-to-five-second delay before it explodes, while the pin on a smoke grenade has no delay. To make the grenade even more deadly, I packed C-4 plastic explosives around the firing device. Then I loosened the pin and tied a trip wire to it. When an enemy soldier tripped the wire it would go off immediately.

Late one afternoon when we were on LZ English, the platoon leader came to me and said the colonel wanted someone to go outside of the perimeter to the site of an OLH-13 helicopter crash. We were flown out just as it was getting dark. In the middle of a huge rice paddy was an OLH-13 that had gone down due to an engine failure. We put straps on it and a Chinook helicopter came out and carried it away.

The colonel came on my radio and said he couldn't get a helicopter out to take us back to English. He wanted us to walk back. We were about five clicks (kilometers) from English, and we were told to move out in the dark. The night had no moon. Because I was the only one with a map, and I knew where we were; I walked point.

We walked about a click, and a covey of birds that were probably some form of quail flew up in front of me. The sound scared me, so I emptied my magazine of eighteen rounds on the birds. Everybody behind me hit the rice paddy. They jumped into the worst kind of mud. It was black and had human excrement mixed in with it. When I told them what happened, I could hear them cursing under their breath. When we got back to English, I stepped aside to count all of them in. Someone had driven a two-and-a-half-ton truck up to the concertina wire and dropped down a large wood plank so we could cross into the perimeter. When I looked at my guys in the light, I could see they were dirty with mud and excrement smeared all over them. My fatigues were as clean as when we started the task. They all had a few choice words to say to me as they filed past.

ONE GREAT COMMANDER

In the early part of November 1967, it was my time for R&R. I flew back to the rear in An Khe and found that someone had used a knife to rip open my duffle bag and steal my Class A uniforms. The supply sergeant helped me scrounge up some khakis, and I went to the PX and bought some Cochran jump boots. On the night before I was to leave for Thailand, my entire company arrived back at An Khe. They were on their way to Dak To. I snapped a black and white picture of them loading their gear into their rucksacks the next morning.

Capt. McDonald had talked to me about replacing the NCO in the rear area as the NCOIC (non commissioned officer in charge) of the rear. So, I thought when I returned to An Khe, I would fly out to the rear supply area and take over. After that, I didn't think much about what I'd be doing next. I left for Qui Nhon where I would catch a plane to Bangkok. I had made contact with Wayne Lynch, my buddy from Germany, to meet up with him in Thailand. I would arrive two days before him, and then we would be together for four or five days.

When I got on the propeller driven airliner to Bangkok, it was like a dream come true. The plane was air-conditioned, and the stewardesses were very pretty. I was told we were having steak and potatoes. I ordered a glass of milk to go with my meal. It was the first glass of milk I had tasted since May. It was cold and tasted great. The flight took about four or five hours to Bangkok.

When we arrived in Bangkok, we were transported to a briefing station at the airport. We were shown a film about the effects of gonorrhea and how to take precautions not to catch it. We were then told what part of town we were not to visit. We were also told we couldn't wear our uniforms out on the town. Then we were assigned to our hotels and put on a bus to take us there. As we stopped at each hotel, there were boys out front who passed bottled beer into our bus. Every bottle was a San Miguel beer. I believe this was the beer partly owned by Gen. Douglas MacArthur's family. We finally arrived at my hotel, and I immediately hired a taxi to drive me to a clothing store.

While I was looking at clothes, someone poured me another beer. On the way back in the taxi, the driver passed me another San Miguel beer. When I got back to my room, I was so dizzy that I lay down on the bed and immediately went to sleep. The next morning I got with someone I had met on the bus. He was a buck sergeant from the 1st Infantry Division named Jeff and his last name started with a "G." We went down for breakfast, and I had a steak. I spent the next several days sightseeing. I took a tour to the bridge over the River Kwai. It was about eighty or ninety miles from Bangkok, so I was gone most of the day.

I toured the Rose Gardens, an immaculate area near where the royal family lived. It was so beautiful. I also bought a tour to Timland. This place was like an amusement park, except it didn't have rides. There were all kinds of shows and entertainment. I let a snake handler wrap a twelve-foot Python around my neck and take a picture. I saw another snake handler in a concrete pit with water running around the edge of it. He had about twenty to twenty-five cobras swimming in the water. He would take a stick with a hook on it and pull them out of the water and slap them in the throat area, and they would immediately rise up and get in the strike position. I thought at the time that I didn't have such a dangerous job after all.

R&R ended all too quickly, and I was on a plane back to Vietnam. When I finally got back to An Khe, there was a note waiting for me at the company orderly room. It was signed by a Capt. Pete Bentson. The note simply read, "Sgt. Warden, get to the field as soon as you receive this note." I didn't know who Bentson was, so I asked the company clerk. He told me Capt. McDonald had been relieved and Capt. Bentson was the new company commander.

There were five new guys in the rear who had just gone through their three-day training program, so I took them with me to the airfield. We hopped a ride on a C-123 to Kontum. I looked around for the company but couldn't find anyone. So I taught the guys who were with me how to construct a hootch out of their rain ponchos. One of the new guys was Earl Osborne. He was from Pineville, N.C. He begged me to see to it that he could come to my squad. We spent the night there and the next morning the rear area personnel and tents arrived via helicopter. They told me the company would be in the next day. The next day I reported to Capt. Bentson and he directed me back to the 3rd platoon. I was back to being a squad leader. When I found out I was a man short in my squad, I requested and got Ozzie to be assigned to my squad.

While I was gone on R&R, our company was around Dak To, and the 3rd platoon came to a small mountain. The platoon leader split up the platoon into two groups to go around both sides of the mountain. When the group, minus the lieutenant, was going around the other side, they spotted a haystack to their front. A Vietnamese was standing near it, and when he spotted them, he dove into the haystack. They ran up and pulled him out of the haystack and rummaged around and pulled out a metal box. The box had several thousand dollars worth of Vietnamese piasters in it.

They were in a quandary. They wanted to keep the money, but if they turned the paymaster they captured in to the authorities, he would tell about the money. If they shot him, the lieutenant would hear the gunshot and question them. So, they decided to kill him another way. First they tried a bayonet, but it was too dull to puncture his chest. They finally dragged him over to a stream and drowned him. They split up the money among themselves and took an oath never to tell about it. I thought about it for a while and decided I was glad I wasn't with them. If I had been, I would have stopped them from killing him.

The next day, we air assaulted out the entire company to the mountains around Dak To. We were taken about halfway up a high mountain just north of Dak To and we started a three-week hike through some of the most treacherous mountain terrain I had ever seen. There were enormous areas devoid of any foliage. The US Air Force had sprayed Agent Orange on the forest around the area to deny the enemy cover. After we moved out of that area, we stayed in triple canopy forest most of the time. We never saw any action, except the point guy for D Company came face to face with our point guy. They couldn't see each other very well, and both emptied their M-16s at each other. Except for a bullet hole in our point guy's pants, they missed each other completely. I was glad of their poor marksmanship.

After our two point men had the shootout with each other, a command came down to us that no one in our infantry company could have a round chambered except for the point man. And the point man had to have his rifle on safety. I can't tell you how stupid we all thought this was. In the dense jungle we were in, the point man could come upon the enemy in an instant. Either the sound of switching the safety off or chambering a round would alert the enemy, or he would be late firing on the enemy. After Capt. Bentson told all of us NCOs about this new order, he asked us to assemble all our men from all the platoons.

He stood in the center of them and in a loud, authoritative voice said, "Men, the higher ups have told us that no one can have a round chambered except the point man!" A loud groan came from nearly everybody. He continued, "But men, I will never check! Does everyone understand?" I thought Bentson handled that about as well as anyone. He was one great commander.

We stayed wet a considerable amount of time in the mountains. It seemed to rain days on end. The leeches attached themselves to us in droves. Every time we took a break, the first thing we did was to check and see how many leeches we had on our bodies. Sometimes I would have over twenty leeches on me. We would get them off by touching a lit cigarette to them or spraying them with our insect repellent. One guy pulled down his pants and discovered a leech had crawled up inside of his penis. He was medevaced and never came back to the field.

We came upon a tunnel complex that began in the middle of a well-worn trail that we were on. Cpl. Barclay, our recon NCO from Bravo Company, 2nd Battalion, 19th Artillery, threw a lighted match down the dark hole, and it immediately blew up. It burned most of the hair from around his face and arms. He had thrown a match on top of a pile of gunpowder. We had to blow an area open in the heavy forest to have a medevac chopper lower a line with a cage to get him out to the hospital.

I remember moving in company formation for days on end in the thickest forest I had ever seen. One day our platoon leader came back from a meeting with Capt. Bentson.

He told me Bentson had told his platoon leaders, "If I had a hundred men like Sgt. Warden, I'd go anywhere in Vietnam!" He wanted to know how and when I had been "brown nosing" Capt. Bentson. I had no idea why Bentson said what he did. After getting to know him better, I took it as a very nice compliment. Capt. Bentson was a graduate of the West Point Class of 1963. He was ranger qualified and a master parachutist. He had been with the 5th Special Forces Group at Fort Bragg before he came to Vietnam. He was one of the best company commanders we ever had in Charlie Company.

I was becoming a super chef when it came to C rations. I would take the white bread that came in a can and place it inside the brown tin foil wrapper that contained the cigarettes, toilet paper, and condiments from the C rations. I would then take a lighter and light the outside wrapper. The brown finish on the outside would catch fire and toast the bread. Then I could mix peanut butter and jelly together for a feast. I melted cheese into the beans and franks, and it tasted a lot better. I made instant coffee and added some cocoa mix.

We used Louisiana Hot Sauce with about everything we ate. It was hard to keep it as far out in the field as we were. One of my guys wrote the Louisiana Hot Sauce people in Louisiana and told them it was our favorite hot sauce. He also told them we had a hard time keeping it in supply. About two weeks later we got four boxes in the mail. Each box contained twenty-four bottles of Louisiana Hot Sauce. Even to this day, my refrigerator always has a bottle of their sauce. After we received the boxes and had a while to think about it, Earl Osborne suggested, "Well, hell, let's write to Jack Daniels and see if they'll send us some bourbon." He did, and they sent us a Clorox bottle of bourbon. When we received the bourbon, we were in a bad area, so I told Ozzie he had to pour it out. I thought he was going to cry, but he did it.

On Thanksgiving Day 1967, we ate Thanksgiving dinner on top of Hill 875 near Dak To. It had been the scene of the worst fighting of the war with the 173rd Airborne losing almost two companies in assaulting this hill. While we were on Hill 875, I ran into two guys from the 173rd who had been in that battle. Before they were transferred to the 173rd, they had been with the 1st of the 12th (1st Battalion, 12th Cavalry). One guy had been in the Army for some time and had taken part in the parachute drop into the Dominican Republic made by the 82nd in the early '60s. We talked about what had happened since they had been transferred out of Charlie Company in September.

About this time, my friend Dennis Rasmussen, who was one of the assistant machine gunners, was stopped by the battalion executive officer on one of the many LZs we were on. Rasmussen had grown a mustache, and the rule was that only staff sergeants and above could have a mustache. The XO promptly ordered Rasmussen to shave it off. Rasmussen had white hair and his mustache just looked like he had been drinking milk. It was hardly noticeable. Being the good "field soldier" that he was, he decided to ignore the order. A couple of days later, the XO caught him again and saw that the mustache was still there. He promptly ordered Dennis back to the rear for charges to be pressed against him.

While in the rear, they couldn't decide where to keep Dennis. They got a Conex container, an all steel structure about the size of a small jail cell, had the motor sergeant cut an opening for ventilation and locked Dennis inside it. He had to yell out to the company clerk whenever he needed to go to the bathroom. The clerk would get his loaded .45 caliber pistol and escort Dennis to the latrine. Dennis would wait until it was late at night and raining hard to ask to go the latrine. He made it as difficult as he could for his captors. After about the third day of this, one of our guys came back from R&R to find Dennis locked up. He asked Dennis if he had consulted with the Judge Advocate (the army's legal organization). Dennis told him, no, he hadn't. This guy went to the JAG office and told them what was going on. Later that day, Rasmussen was released to go back to the field, with no charges filed against him. It was one of the most outrageous miscarriages of justice I ever witnessed in the army.

Rasmussen didn't care, though. He was just glad to get three days of rest away from the field. When he returned to the field, we all had a good laugh about it.

PART V:
BATTLE OF TAM QUAN

BO'S SHOT!

We returned to Bong Son from Dak To on the afternoon of December 14th and were immediately air assaulted from LZ English to just north of Bong Son. We landed close to where our episode with the booby-trapped ruins in the sand had claimed Ashley and the others as casualties.

Cliff Metz was on R&R, so Dennis Rasmussen was on one gun and Rick Boeshart was carrying the other machine gun. We walked west several kilometers and received our hot meal via chow choppers in the heat of the afternoon. We moved on west and encountered tall palm groves and hedgerows that went everywhere.

I won't name the sergeant whose turn it was to do ambush for the evening, but I will tell you what I thought about him. Anytime I was acting platoon sergeant, he complained about my being picked to be platoon sergeant over him. He was an RA (regular army) NCO, and he told me that constantly. I thought he was stupid and couldn't think beyond the end of his nose. I remember one night in the mountains, I told him to have his squad dig foxholes, and he told me to dig them myself. I came down from where I had been eating C rations and told him in a raised voice that if he didn't comply, I was going to beat him to a pulp in front of his men. I was a head taller than him, and he backed down. He belatedly complied with my order. That night we drew mortar rounds and some of his men thanked me later for making them dig in.

Anyway, it was his turn to pull ambush with his squad. He had a small squad—not over four guys—and the platoon leader told me to loan him a few of my men. I told the platoon leader in a heated tone that I was not going to loan him any of my guys. I didn't trust him, and I wouldn't let my guys be endangered by being under his leadership. The exchange was becoming heated. I offered to pull the ambush with my squad, but I was adamant that I was not going to loan him any of my guys. Boeshart, who was the new squad leader for the weapons squad, spoke up and said he would go on ambush with the sergeant and his squad. He probably helped me avoid a court-martial. Bo, Charlie Waskey, and Larry Heath accompanied the other squad that night.

The next morning we had coffee and whatever we could come up with for chow. We moved out about eight o'clock in the morning and formed a sweeping formation with the 1st and 2nd platoons in the middle, the 4th platoon on the left flank and the 3rd platoon (my platoon) on the right flank. Capt. Pete Benson was directly behind the 1st and 2nd platoons with his CP.

We hadn't gone two hundred meters, when over to our far left we heard automatic gunfire and a lot of it. We didn't have much time to think about it though, because about that same time all hell broke loose to our right front. We hit the dirt and returned fire as best we could. We peered into the foliage but couldn't see anyone straight ahead. It was because the 22nd NVA Regiment was dug into our front with elaborate, networked trenches covering several acres.

Then we were hit from our right flank. This time we could see the NVA in their khaki uniforms, pith helmets, and weapons. In addition, a number of soldiers with them were dressed in green fatigues. When I saw the fatigues the same color as ours, I hesitated, but when I saw them pointing weapons in our direction, I opened fire, and so did everybody else. I looked to my left and saw Boeshart with Waskey and Heath laying down suppressing fire toward the enemy. We were in a major firefight in a matter of seconds.

Then the enemy assault started. About ten or eleven NVA came running toward us, firing wildly. I put my M-16 on semi-automatic and fired at perhaps six or seven of them. I know I hit everybody that I fired at during those moments, but not one of the NVA went down. One ran up to within ten feet of me, and I emptied the rest of my magazine into him. He stopped, turned around, and walked back toward the hedgerow where he came from and disappeared, while I changed magazines for my rifle. When he turned away from me, I could see huge splotches of blood on his back where the rounds from my M-16 had exited his body.

We repelled the attack without anyone being hit or wounded. Not one of the NVA broke through our lines. I told everyone to make sure they had magazines handy because I expected them to try it again. At that very moment, bursts of automatic weapon fire erupted to our rear. My platoon leader told me to pull my squad back and go to our rear to repel any attacks coming from the rear. My squad and I ran about one hundred meters to the rear and were immediately pinned down. I could hear shouts coming from what I thought was the enemy, but it sounded like English. I looked over the sand dune I was behind and drew several rounds aimed at my head.

I raised my rifle and started shouting, "Hey, we're Americans! Hold your fire!" The firing stopped, and when I could do so without fearing for my life, I rose to my knees. About seventy meters from my position were American GIs. They were from Delta Company, 1st of the 12th, our sister company. Delta Company had an RTO, Alan Lynch, who was awarded the Medal of Honor for his actions later that day.

Assured that we weren't getting hit from the rear, I took my squad and started to return to our position in the formation. We ran into our platoon leader almost immediately. After he sent me and my squad to the rear, he ordered a pullback for the platoon. He left just Boeshart and his gun crew to cover the retreat. As they pulled back, another human wave attack came and in the withering fire, Bo took rounds to his chest and throat.

Waskey immediately began shouting, "Bo's shot—Bo's shot! Medic! Medic!" I heard this, and all my guys followed me out to where Bo lay slumped, face down. Waskey and Heath had all they could handle manning the gun. I had not noticed that Spec. 5th Class Tom Jensen, our medic, had followed us out to Bo and his gun crew. Tom turned Bo over and ripped his shirt open.

As we watched, another assault came from the NVA to our front and left flank. I usually carried thirty-six magazines (almost three hundred rounds) and five grenades with me at all times. At this point, I didn't have any grenades, and I was almost out of ammo. I turned around and saw that Doc Jensen was down. He had been up on his knees administering mouth-to-mouth to Bo, when he was hit across the chest several times with bullets. I crawled over to them and saw Bo was not breathing. Doc Jensen was screaming. I directed two of my guys to take Doc back to rear to the CP and get him medevaced. Doc Jensen was one of the bravest guys I knew. He was a conscientious objector. I don't know if it was for religious or personal reasons. But I know he was always with us during the bad times, and he didn't carry a weapon. There was no way I would have been in the bush without a weapon.

Then David Wilkowski was hit in the ankle with shrapnel. I didn't have anybody left to help him, so I put his arm over my shoulder and helped him to the medevac chopper. We crossed about 150 yards of open terrain to get there. As I looked down, I saw bullets kicking up the sand all around my feet.

I got Wilkowski on the helicopter, turned, and ran back to where I left my guys, Waskey, and Heath. Our platoon leader, who was now safely to our rear about one hundred meters, hollered at me to get out of there. I knew Bo was dead and there was nothing we could do for him. I ordered everybody to pull back to the platoon leader. We used scrambling fire to get everybody back safely. The front guy pulls through the group while they lay down cover fire for him; then the front guy comes through in like fashion until we were far enough back for everyone to run back to the rest of the platoon. It was a maneuver I had insisted on practicing.

We hadn't been back to the rest of the platoon five minutes when Waskey came to me and blamed the platoon leader for leaving them out in front all exposed and alone to cover his and the rest of the platoon's retreat. I didn't have time to think about it then. We were still in the biggest firefight I had ever experienced.

WOUNDED

I found out Sgt. Merritt's weapons platoon on our left
flank had walked into an ambush. They had lost six of their
men in the ambush and spent most of the day trying to
get to them. My friend, Spec. 4th Class Perry Benally, a
Navajo Indian, was in the 4th platoon. He had been one
of the six who walked right into a major fortification of
the NVA. The NVA waited until they were right on top
of them before they opened fire. Perry and I met the next
day in the 15th Evac Hospital at Bong Son where he told
me his story. I felt it best to let you read his story from two
sources. One, as told to Spec. Richard Hawkins, who wrote
an aricle about Perry for the Cavalair, a newspaper from the
Information Office of the 1st Cav, and the other from the
Stars and Stripes.

Soldier Survives 'Ordeal By Fire'

By SP4 RICHARD HAWKINS
Cavalair Staff Writer

BONG SON — In a soft voice, showing little emotion, Specialist Four Perrie V. Benallie told how he and his buddies from the 1st Air Cavalry Division's 1st Battalion, 12th Cavalry were advancing through palm groves and hedges into a fortified village where a patrol had been fired on earlier in the morning.

Enemy sniper rounds began to crack around them as they moved into the village. Fragments from an enemy rifle grenade tore into Benallie's right leg. "But it didn't hurt much so I just kept on going," he said. His platoon was moving toward a hedgerow when it erupted in fire from enemy automatic weapons.

As Benallie tried to get in position to fire back and hopefully cover a withdrawal, a machine

Additional Tam Quan Photos, Story Page 8

gun bullet creased his right temple. "It just stung," he said, gesturing toward his bandaged head.

'Couldn't Signal'

Driven back by the heavy fire, the company regrouped for another assault on the enemy. Though they were able to reach two other wounded men in a shallow ditch 20 feet behind Benallie, they could not cross the open area to the small depression where he lay. "I couldn't signal to them," he said, "or they (the NVA) would have opened up on me again."

A third assault, this time supported by tracked armored personnel carriers (APC's) from the Cav's 1st Battalion, 50th Mechanized Infantry, was still unable to reach Benallie's position. One of the vehicles was disabled by an enemy recoilless rifle as it rumbled to within 15 feet of the wounded soldier. The sun had set and darkness was fast approaching.

Emptied M-16

Taking his rifle, he began crawling back to the ditch where his two buddies had been

rescued earlier. On the way he saw two NVA soldiers step from behind a hut barely 20 feet away. "I emptied a magazine (20 rounds) at them," said Benallie. He believed he had killed both of them.

Reaching the ditch, he found a U.S. pistol belt and a grenade left behind by the troops who had been there. Knowing that his rifle had announced his presence to the enemy, he threw the grenade back to his original position and used the explosion to cover his further escape.

Crawling down a trail looking for a place to hide, he spotted a small hole. As he came close to it, "another one stuck his head out and looked at me. I just swing my rifle as hard as I could at his head. I hit him twice."

No Delay

Not waiting around to see if there was any fight left in his adversary, Benallie took off again, this time on the run.

"Finally I saw a grave," he said. It was a Vietnamese farmer's grave, a mound of packed earth encircled by a stone wall. He found the inside partially overgrown with bushes and curled up inside them next to the wall for cover.

Enemy rifle fire and grenades were still coming from the village behind him. One rifle grenade landed near his shelter, peppering the wall with shrapnel. But soon the enemy fire was silenced by U.S. artillery. By this time three infantry companies and two APC companies were in position around the village. Most of an NVA regiment was trapped.

Big Guns

The big guns from the nearby U.S. fire bases poured hundreds of rounds into the enemy positions during the night. Shrapnel fell inside the stone wall, but its velocity was spent and it did no damage. Benallie, lying cold, wounded and alone in the target area, couldn't sleep. "All I could do was (Continued on Back Page)

(Continued on Back Page)

Ordeal By Fire—

(Continued from Page 1)

pray," he said.

When the artillery barrage stopped for a moment the enemy fire would resume. "They still knew I was out there somewhere," Benallie said.

Both the artillery and small arms fire had died down by morning, when Benallie heard the drone of U.S. spotter planes overhead. "I stood up and held up my helmet and waved my dog tags at them, but they didn't see me," he said. The planes were there to mark targets for Air Force fighter-bombers. Soon 750-pound bombs were pounding the area, their cracking explosions shaking the ground and sending hot metal fragments whining through the air.

Heard APC's

The battle began again a short time later, with rifles and machine guns throwing bullets over his head. He could hear APC's coming toward him, backed by the infantry. "One was coming real close, but I didn't think they would see me so I rolled over and waved and shouted, 'Over here! Over here!'"

Sp4 Benallie doesn't know who found him. But they recognized him and took him back to a secure area where a medical evacuation helicopter picked him up for a flight to an aid station and treatment.

Benallie was rescued on his 22nd birthday.

From the clean sheets of his hospital bed in Qui Nhon he said, "You know, this is the first time I've been in a hospital in my life."

An Army doctor came to visit him on his morning rounds and Benallie showed him the Purple Heart Medal.

What could the doctor say except, "You sure earned it."

GI Can Celebrate: He's 22, Alive

BONG SON, Vietnam (IO)—In a soft voice, Spec. 4 Perrie V. Benallie tells how he and his buddies from the 1st Air Cav. Div.'s 1st Bn., 12th Cav., were advancing through palm groves and hedges into a fortified village where a patrol had been fired on earlier.

Enemy sniper fire began to crack around them as they moved in.

Fragments from an enemy rifle grenade tore into Benallie's right leg. "It didn't hurt much so I just kept on going," he said.

His platoon was moving toward a hedgerow when enemy automatic weapons opened up.

As Benallie tried to get in position to return fire and hopefully cover a withdrawal, a machine gun bullet creased his right temple. "It just stung," he said, gesturing toward his bandaged head.

Driven back by the heavy fire, the company regrouped. They were able to reach two other wounded men in a ditch 20 feet behind Benallie, but they couldn't cross the open area to where he lay. "I couldn't signal to them," he said,

"or the enemy would have opened up again."

A third assault, this time supported by armored personnel carriers from the Cav.'s 1st Bn., 50th Mechanized Inf., also was unable to reach Benallie. One of the vehicles was disabled by an enemy recoilless rifle as it rumbled to within 15

(Continued on Back Page, Col. 1)

GI Is 22—and Alive

(Continued From Page 1)

feet of the wounded soldier. Darkness was approaching fast now.

Taking his rifle, Benallie began crawling back to the ditch where his two buddies had been rescued earlier. Two North Vietnamese soldiers stepped from behind a but hardly 20 feet away. "I emptied a magazine at them," Benallie said. He thinks he killed both of them.

Reaching the ditch, he found a pistol belt and grenade left behind. He threw the grenade and used the explosion as cover.

Crawling down a trail looking for a place to hide, he spotted a small hole. As he came close to it, "another one stuck his head out and looked at me. I swung my rifle as hard as I could at his head. I hit him twice."

Benallie took off again, this time on the run.

"Finally I saw a grave," he said, a mound of packed earth enclosed by a stone wall. The inside was partially overgrown with bushes. Benallie curled up next to the wall for cover.

Enemy fire was still coming from the village. A rifle grenade landed near his shelter, peppering the wall with shrapnel. The enemy fire was finally silenced by U.S. artillery. By this time three infantry and two APC companies were positioned around the village. Most of the

NVA regiment was trapped.

Big guns from nearby U.S. fire bases poured hundreds of rounds into the enemy positions during the night. Shrapnel fell inside Benallie's stone wall, but it was spent and did no damage. Benallie was lying cold, wounded and alone. "All I could do was pray," he said.

When the artillery barrage stopped momentarily, the enemy fire would resume. "They still knew I was out there somewhere," Benallie said.

The artillery and small arms fire died down by morning. Then Benallie heard the drone of U.S. spotter planes overhead. "I stood and held up my helmet and waved but they didn't see me," he said. The planes were there to mark targets for Air Force fighter-bombers. Soon 750-pound bombs were pounding the area, their explosions shaking the ground.

The battle began again a short time later. Benallie could hear APCs coming toward him, backed by the infantry. "One was coming real close, but I didn't think they would see me so I rolled over and waved and shouted. 'Over here! Over here!'"

Benallie doesn't know who found him. He was taken to a secure area where a medical evacuation helicopter picked him up.

It wasn't a bad present for Benallie—on his 22nd birthday.

After Waskey talked to me about blaming the platoon leader for leaving them exposed, it started to sink in that I, or rather we, had just lost one of our best friends. I lost count of how many times we had rounds shot at us, when I would look to my side and Bo would be there. He would look at me and ask, "Doug, where do you want rounds?" I always knew he would put the rounds out, and he would put them where I wanted them. I just never worried when Bo was around. He and Cliff Metz, the other gunner in our platoon, were cut from the same cloth. The more I thought about it, the more I felt really bad.

And Bo's body was still lying out there. I knew he would come after me if the situation were reversed. I got my squad together and looked each of them in the eye.

I said, "I'm going after Bo. Anybody want to go with me?" Everybody nodded in agreement. This was something I couldn't order them to do. You don't order people to go under fire to retrieve the dead. So, Gouley, Osborne, Morgan, Hayes, and I went to get Bo's body. We made the trip without anybody getting killed or wounded. We drew lots of enemy fire; I saw the sand kick up all around us. The entire trip was made under heavy fire. We brought his body back and laid it with the others from the 4th platoon who had been killed.

All of us knew that many personal items never made it back to the family from the graves registration process, so I took Bo's billfold and rosary beads. . I later sent them to his family. I was heartbroken. As I was kneeling and crying over Bo's body, I looked up, and I saw an Army photographer taking pictures of me. I went after him, yanked the camera out of his hands, and threw it on the ground. I tried to break it by stomping on it, but I just ground it into the sand. When my first attempt failed, I emptied a full magazine into the camera. I looked at the dumbstruck army photographer. He didn't say a word. I thought, "*How dare he invade my privacy and disrespect the dead?*" To this day, the only people I despise more than lawyers are news photographers and news people.

We then assembled for an assault on the NVA positions directly to our front. My squad was put on the right flank of the entire company's assault line. Several APCs from the 1st Battalion, 50th Infantry, had joined us. We got on line and began our assault. We were all walking about five to six meters apart and firing at anything that even remotely looked like the enemy. The APCs were firing their .50 caliber machine guns from just behind where the APC commander stood. We heard a loud boom to our left, and I saw both the APC commander, and the machine gunner disappear from view. They had taken a direct hit from an RPG.

Spec. 4th Class Wayne Ryza from our platoon ran up behind the APC and opened the door to try to help any survivors he could find. Just as he got the door open, another round was launched at the center of the APC; it passed through and hit him in the chest. I looked just in front of the APC and saw the enemy soldier who hit the APC. He was in a trench with the RPG in his hands. I yelled to Phillip Hayes to start putting M-79 grenade rounds at that position. I shouted to all who could hear that I was going out front of our assault line, so they wouldn't take a shot at me. Someone had to get to that enemy soldier before he could fire again at the other APCs. I crawled forward to flank the guy and get a shot at him. I rose up just enough to see him. He was re-armed with a round on his RPG and looking toward another APC. I raised my weapon and aimed at his head. I dropped him with one shot. Now my problem was how to get back without getting shot by my own guys.

I got out of there by keeping my head down below the top of the trench. When I got back to where Hayes was, I shouted at him to tell everyone that I was out front and coming in.

He said, "Good shooting, Doug!" It felt good to have relieved the heavy fire on those APCs. Capt. Bentson screamed over at me that he had ordered everyone to cease fire. I meekly told him that I had just shot the guy who had wiped out the APC. It was a sickening feeling to see those guys disappear from sight when they were hit. I knew several soldiers in the APC were killed or hurt and that Ryza was probably dead. As we advanced some more, we took on even more heavy fire. Word came to pull back, so we could re-group. Day was turning to dusk. I hadn't realized it, but we had been in constant contact now for over ten hours.

I walked back to the platoon and was told I was now platoon sergeant. Sgt. Campbell had been wounded and medevaced. I made Buster Morgan squad leader for my squad, and I began to give orders for our positions for the night. I had thrown over fifteen grenades and had fired over one hundred magazines of ammo on December 15th. The rest of my guys had reloaded every magazine they carried over three times. The re-supply helicopters were great that day. They hovered right over us while drawing fire, and kicked out the boxes of ammo and water right on top of our positions.

Sometime during the fight on the 15th, our company commander Capt. Benson had injured his knee seriously.

His knee swelled up the size of a football. I later learned he had injured it playing football at West Point and had kept the injury a secret, so it would not jeopardize his army career. His time in the field was over. It was certainly our loss. He was the finest company commander I ever served under.

That night, I was behind the perimeter I had set up for the platoon. I was up all night as we drew sporadic small arms fire. The enemy managed to get close to our lines that night, because the next morning we could see fresh punji stakes pointed toward our lines. Early that morning, all of us up and down the line were told to "pop smoke" for the F-4 jets that were firing twenty mm cannons, dropping napalm and 750-pound bombs.

At this point, our platoon leader was gone. I don't remember if he was medevaced or what happened to him. I don't even remember whether he left on the evening of the 15th or the morning of the 16th. I just know that on the morning of the 16th, I was the platoon leader. I went up to the CP, where Lt. Denny Lentsch had replaced Capt. Benson as the CO. He was briefing us on the size of the enemy, how we were going to assault, who was going to be where, where the medevac spot would be located—all those things that need to be coordinated before a firefight. As he talked, a couple of helicopters landed about fifty meters to our rear with a couple of groups of new guys on board. We got about ten to fifteen replacements to fill in where we had lost people.

Just as they approached Lt. Lentsch, the F-4s started yet another bombing run. They began dropping 750-pounders. Dirt, tree branches and brush began falling all around us.

We went down on our stomachs and kept our heads down to avoid injury. Lentsch began to talk to these new guys whose eyes were as big around as silver dollars. I looked at one and tears were streaming down his face. I thought to myself, *"I'm so glad I had at least two days before I had my initiation by fire!"*

Lentsch assigned about three or four of the new guys to me. I took them down to where I was set up and told them, "Look, I've been out here six months, and I've never lost a man. I'm not going to assign you to a squad, because you'll just get in the way and get hurt. You guys stick with me, and I'll get you through this." They didn't say a word; they just shook their heads with grateful looks on their faces. By keeping them with me, they were no safer. They would be only ten to fifteen feet behind the assault line. But they didn't know that, and perhaps it gave them some comfort. As I remember it, the new guys were Pfc. Jerry Richards, Pfc. Joe Bonetti, Pfc. David Kipfinger, and Pfc. Paul Wachter.

We waited for an hour or so as the jets kept coming in at tremendous speeds, dropping their ordinance just thirty or so meters from where we were held up. I gave the operations order and the time for our assault to the squad leaders in the 3rd platoon. When we stood up and began our assault, we went a few dozen meters and were pinned down by small arms fire. I saw someone up in front of me draw a bead on a figure up against a wall in front of us. I screamed at him, "Don't shoot! He's one of ours!" I recognized Spec. 4th Class Benally who had been wounded the day before. When he couldn't get back to the platoon, he had hid overnight in the bushes on a Vietnamese farmer's grave. A couple of guys in gas masks ran up to him and started dragging him to the rear. I stopped in a huge bomb crater with Billy Cabaniss, my RTO, and the new guys, who were following me like little puppies.

Lentsch called on the radio to all the platoon leaders to have their platoons pop smoke to mark their forward progress for the jets. They were going to call in another air strike. I had a smoke grenade on my web gear, so I stood up to throw it out in front of our position. When I was at the top of my throw, I went down like a pin hit by a bowling ball. I found myself looking up at the blue sky with a hurt in my chest that felt like a heavyweight boxer had punched me on my sternum with all his force. I had been wearing two bandoleers of extra machine gun ammo for the machine gunners, one over each shoulder. They had both split into two. I put my hand to my chest where it hurt. When I lifted my hand, it was covered in blood.

I immediately started praying to God to forgive me for all my sins. Then I thought of how my mother was going to take my death. My thought was that she would never be the same. Someone must have called for a medic, because I looked up to see Joe "Doc" O'Keefe looking down at me. He was removing the plastic packaging from a bandage.

He put the plastic wrapper on my chest (it's used for a sucking chest wound when the lung is punctured) and said to me, "Hang on, Doug, I'll try to save you!" That confirmed my worst fear. I was dying, and there was no hope. Doc used his fingers to pry a AK 47 round from my breastbone. He took the bullet and put it in my fatigue shirt pocket. He said, "Keep this. You'll have something to show to your grandkids!" The M-60 rounds that I had been wearing had slowed the bullet down enough to be stopped by my sternum.

I looked up at the new guys who were white as ghosts looking down at me. I couldn't talk for the pain, so I didn't even try to calm their fears. Pieces from the ammo belts I was wearing had pierced the right hand of one of the new guys, Jerry Richards, and he was bleeding. An APC backed up to the bomb crater I was in. They picked me up, threw me in, and closed the door. The ceiling door was open, so I could see pretty well. I looked around and saw that even though there were about six other guys in the APC, I was the only one still alive.

After I was medevaced, Dennis Rasmussen, one of our machine gunners, was in a hole with one of the new guys, David Kipfinger. Kipfinger was pretty wired from all the action he had seen so far. Dennis decided to try to calm him down. He told Kipfinger, "I'm going to close my eyes for a bit and rest. I suggest you do the same." Rasmussen closed his eyes and in a few minutes was sound asleep. He was not really trying to go to sleep, he was just trying to calm Kipfinger down. Dennis woke up after about 15 minutes and continued on with the fight.

DEALING WITH GRIEF

We got back to the rear area near the CP, where the mede-vac choppers were flying in every few minutes. I was lying there when the first sergeant came up to me and offered me a cigarette. I refused because I thought I had a hole in my lung. A few minutes later, they loaded me onto the heli-copter with another guy from another company, who had a severed femoral artery. I was out of the firefight after more than thirty straight hours. The other guy died on the way to the 15th Medical unit at LZ English.

The helicopter landed near the tents of the 15th Medical Detachment. I was carried by stretcher to a cot in one of the tents. The army doctor who treated me pulled out a sliver of brass from an unexploded M-60 round from my chest and used a black plastic clamp or butterfly suture to secure the wound. I was dumbfounded. Surely, someone who was about to die at least deserved a big bandage and stitches. The doctor informed me I was not wounded seri-ously, although I would have a big bruise on my chest for a while. The round had hit square in the center of the two ammunition belts I was wearing around my shoulders and became implanted in my breastbone. It had also driven a sliver of an M-60 round into my chest that caused all of the bleeding and pain. He then put a Band-Aid over the clamp and told me I was fine to return to duty. I felt like I had received a new lease on life. I saw Perry Benally in the tent. He looked pretty bad. He was on a cot all bandaged up. I told him I had recognized him during our assault and stopped someone from shooting him. He was medevaced out, and I never saw him again. He was a good soldier and a credit to his Native American people. I hope he is doing well.

I walked from the 15th Med to our rear area. When I walked into the tent, the guys who were there almost fainted. They had reported me as KIA (killed in action). When they heard over the radio that one of the wounded on the helicopter had died, they mistakenly thought it was me. They had my rifle and my backpack, so I gathered them up and told them I would go back out on the chow chopper later in the day.

I walked over to the brigade TOC and saw Capt. Radcliffe, who was now the brigade S-3 operations officer. He seemed overjoyed to see me. He wasn't half as glad as I was to see him. As I was filling him in on what had happened over the course of the last two days, Col. Rattan walked in. Radcliffe introduced me to the colonel. He asked me about what had been happening. He was especially interested to hear that a few of the NVA were wearing green fatigues in the battle. We surmised at the time that they were probably Chinese advisors. There had been rumors for quite some time that Chinese troops were seen with the NVA.

After talking with Radcliffe a while longer, I returned to our tent. I caught the chow chopper out to Tam Quan that afternoon. When I arrived, the first sergeant almost fell over. He, too, had heard I was dead. My platoon was out on a sweep to gather up enemy equipment and make a body count of the enemy. When they returned, it was like old home week. They made over me in a big way and were glad to know I wasn't KIA. One of my guys wanted to see the bandage from my wounds. I reluctantly showed him my Band-Aid, and he and the other guys started to laugh.

"Aw, Doug, we thought you were hurt!" Although we all found humor in it after the fact, it wasn't very funny when it was happening.

In this chapter, I have included two more articles about the battle of Tam Quan from the 1st Cav's newspaper, *Cavalair.* There were more articles about the battle, but I included these to give you a sense of the importance that our leaders and the news media gave to this battle. We all thought at the time that we surprised the enemy as they were getting into position for the Tet Offensive of 1968. Of all the major cities in Vietnam, Bong Son had no major offensive directed against it during Tet. I think we crippled the enemy's plans as the result of this battle.

Cav Medic Aids Ambushed Squad

BONG SON — The field medic in Vietnam has one of the most difficult and dangerous jobs in the Army.

They walk where the infantrymen walk, carry a larger pack than anyone except a radio operator, and, when a battle breaks out, its their job to go where the action is — to find the wounded and patch them up.

That was the job of Specialist Four Joseph W. O'Keefe when Charlie Company of the 1st Air Cavalry Division's 1st Battalion, 12th Cavalry helped write a chapter in the Battle of Tam Quan.

Ambushed

Six men in Charlie Company were ambushed by NVA (North Vietnamese Army) regulars and the rest of the company, trying to rescue the ambushed squad, found themselves in an intense firefight.

While bullets flew, Doc O'Keefe made his rounds.

"The NVA really had us outflanked," O'Keefe said. "I couldn't get to the six ambushed men but we had quite a few others wounded and that kept me busy." Three men walking behind a 1st Battalion, 50th Infantry (Mechanized) track were hit by an NVA sniper and a nearby medic ran over to help them.

Opened Fire

"They were really pouring out the bullets," said O'Keefe. "But I was finally able to get to the men and drag them behind a track. I got them patched up alright and got them inside the track and we called in a medevac."

O'Keefe spotted another man hit as he raced across the battlefield. "He had a belly wound and I patched him up as well as I could. The guy started to go. He probably had internal bleeding, but after I gave him a shot of albumin he came back."

A medevac ship was called in to take out the man, but both he and O'Keefe were too close to the front lines. "When that medevac chopper came in," said Private First Class Eddie Hardee, Charlie Company's forward observer, "these NVA really opened up. They were trying to knock it out of the sky."

Stretcher Sent

One of the gunners on the medevac ship kicked out a stretcher and O'Keefe called three other men to help him. They placed the wounded man on the stretcher and, with enemy bullets splashing around them, they carried the man some 100 meters to a waiting medevac ship.

Once he helped the man aboard, O'Keefe hurried back to the battlefield.

"When they saw Doc," Hardee said, "they opened up again. He finally made it to three wounded men and pulled them into a trench. He tried to bandage them but each time he would reach up to apply a patch, the NVA would catch sight of his first-aid pack and fire at him. Finally Doc just said 'To hell with the NVA' and he patched up the men."

Recoilless Rifle

When the tracks received some heavy recoilless rifle fire, knocking out one track, killing one man and wounding three others, they pulled back for artillery. ARA, and jet strikes, O'Keefe pulled back with them.

Jets pounded the area with 750-pound bombs for two solid hours. When the tracks and 1/12th soldiers assaulted again they met no resistance.

O'Keefe turned to help the wounded men aboard the medevac ships. The next morning Charlie Company had two more men wounded by sniper fire. O'Keefe was there again to patch them up.

'Charmed Life'

"He lives a charmed life," one of the men said. Hardee agreed. "He did a tremendous job. He was running all over the field, helping our wounded men and really leaving himself out in the open. And when those NVA saw his medical supplies, they would open up on him."

"These men were great," O'Keefe said. "Once they saw their own men getting hit, there was no stopping them. Of the six men ambushed, two were killed and two were wounded. The other two, not hit, could have escaped but chose to stay with the wounded men."

The Battle of Tam Quan
APC's, Jet Airstrikes
Pound Enemy Bunkers

By SP4 MIKE LARSON
Cavalair Staff Writer

BONG SON — Flashes of the setting sun came through the trees as the men of the 1st Cav made their way through the war-torn field.

Smoke still rising from broken and charred tree trunks and palm leaves burned their nostrils. Cocoanut trees lay strewn across the field, trunks frayed by shrapnel, split and cracked cocoanuts scattered about by huge explosions. An occasional piece of black clothing rolled along the soft dirt.

Two dead steers lay beside a huge crater where a 750-pound bomb had landed. A sow wandered aimlessly through the debris, followed by eight little pigs.

Probes Village

The 1st Air Cavalry Division's 1st Battalion, 12th Cavalry was walking across a battlefield, a small piece of land in central South Vietnam where the enemy had been forced to stand and fight.

A six-man squad had probed this area near the village of My An, four miles north of Bong Son, after North Vietnamese Army snipers fired on an OH-13 observation helicopter. The six men spotted a sniper in a treetop and moved to flank him. All of a sudden, a solid volley of fire burst out from their front and their flanks. Two of the U.S. soldiers were killed, two wounded, and two men, who might have pulled back but chose to stay with the wounded, were not hit. Much of the fighting to follow was centered around these men.

The remainder of the company tried to rescue the ambushed squad, but heavy NVA fire drove them back.

APC's Used

Armored personnel carriers of the 1st Cav's 1st Battalion, 50th Infantry (Mechanized) joined the 1/12th to assault the NVA positions.

But the NVA, dug in more than six feet behind a hedgerow, had recoilless rifles. One track took two rounds, which killed one and wounded three men. "One round went right through the front, right through the engine, right through the cab," said Specialist 4 Michael Crab-

tree, of the 11th Pathfinder Company, working with the 1st of the 12th.

NVA automatic weapons opened up again as the American units pulled back, leaving behind one platoon that was pinned down when they tried to rescue the six men who had been ambushed.

Only when jets brought in 750-pound bombs did enemy firepower fizzle.

"It was frustrating," said PFC Eddie Hardee, a forward artillery observer. "Our artillery was right on target, and the NVA just kept firing. But when those jets dropped bombs for two hours, they literally blew this area away. Every five to eight seconds you could hear bombs going off."

CO Comments

When the APCs and the 1st of the 12th troopers assaulted again, they met no resistance.

Lieutenant Colonel Daniel French, 1st of the 12th commander who took control of one company during the battle when it lost its commanding officer, talked with the men. "A detainee has told us who we were fighting," French said. "You were fighting the Seventh and Eighth NVA Battalions, the 22nd Regimental Headquarters, the 132nd Signal Company, and the 135th Recoilless Rifle Company. That's 900 people."

"Some of the bravery exhibited with fire coming from all sides," French added, "was unbelievable. You came through like champs."

After I returned to my platoon, we were ordered back to the rear at Bong Son. We had lost so many killed and wounded that we couldn't stay in the field. We showered, shaved, ate, and slept inside the wire around the company tent at LZ English. The next day we were ordered to pull perimeter guard around the helipads adjacent to LZ English for the 227th Aviation wing.

They held a memorial service for those who had perished on December 15th and 16th. Even though I felt a great sense of loss over Rick Boeshart and Wayne Ryza, I couldn't bring myself to attend. I stayed in somebody's tent while the service was going on. I did anything to take my mind off what had happened. The memorial service was for Sgt. Richard J. Boeshart, Cpl. Richard A. "Doc" Choppa, Staff Sgt David P. Jewell, Pfc. James J. Koprivnidar, Sgt. 1st Class Robert Levine, Sgt. 1st Class James E. Lynn, Cpl. Steven Matarazzo, Sgt. 1st Class John D. Roche, Spec. 4th Class Wayne Ryza, and Cpl. Mike Sander. The mood in the 3rd platoon was very somber. My entire time in Vietnam, I never witnessed one soldier's death that affected so many men, but Boeshart's death bothered everyone. We all felt like we had lost a brother. Rich Valles, one of my friends from the platoon had told me that he had felt, up until Bo's death, that there were two indestructible guys in our platoon, Boeshart and me. Bo was one terrific machine gunner, but he was also one terrific friend and brother.

While we were pulling palace guard for the aviation guys, one of the new soldiers who came into my platoon came to me asking to speak to the chaplain. It seems ridiculous now, thinking back on this incident. Here was this new guy who had paid for sex and "fallen in love" with one of the prostitutes who worked in one of the bars outside the wire, and now he wanted to get married. I really took all of my frustrations out on him. I told him just how stupid his request sounded. In a very loud voice, I told him he could not see the chaplain under any circumstances, and I promptly assigned him to KP to keep him away from the bar that was just outside the wire fence that separated us from the village nearby. I thought that I kept him from making a very bad mistake. I don't even know if the chaplain would have intervened for him, but I never let it get that far.

The next day, Lt. Col. French drove up in front of my tent and ordered me into his jeep. On the way downtown to Bong Son, he told me that three of my men were in a lot of trouble. MPs had surrounded them and were going to have to use force to arrest them unless we could calm the situation down. When we got to the bar where this incident was unfolding, I saw Charlie Waskey, Duane McAndrews, and David Wilkowski backed into a corner of an open air bar. There were tables and chairs strewn everywhere. It looked like a hurricane had blown through.

My three guys had gone downtown to drink when they were restricted to LZ English. Infantrymen were the only soldiers who were allowed to go downtown with weapons. So all three of them were armed with M-16s, and I believe Waskey had a .45 caliber pistol. An MP lieutenant walked in to the bar and told them it was off limits and they would have to move on. Most of the time when we were downtown, the MPs wouldn't mess with us, even when we were a little bit loud. They knew it was dangerous to mess with infantrymen who were armed and drinking.

This particular lieutenant didn't seem to understand the danger he was in. When Waskey, McAndrews, and Wilkowski wouldn't leave, he drew his pistol. McAndrews promptly took the pistol away from him and proceeded to break it down as if to clean it. As he took it apart, he threw each piece as far as he could into the bushes near the road. The lieutenant left without a word, but he returned in about thirty minutes with two jeeploads of MPs. The MPs drew their weapons and the three infantrymen drew theirs. One of the MPs did get Waskey's pistol away from him and three of the MPs promptly jumped him to get him to the ground. What none of us knew—and certainly not the MPs—was that Waskey held a black belt in karate. He whirled, threw several punches, and put all three of the MPs who had jumped him on the ground. They were now at a standstill.

That's when we arrived. Col. French gave me an order to have my men disarm themselves. I walked up to them and in a soft voice told them I was taking their weapons. I got the two M-16s from McAndrews and Wilkowski and told Waskey to stand down and allow himself to be arrested. I accompanied Col. French to the MP station back at LZ English. They released all three to Col. French and soon we were standing in front of his desk. He looked like Andy Devine from the old black and white movies, but he certainly didn't sound like him. He dismissed all three of my men with an Article 15 without loss of rank and confined them to the company area for thirty days. The confinement was really a joke since we were due to go back outside the wire in a day or two. He really let them off easy.

After those three left his office, he started in on me. He told me that if any of my men got into trouble again, he would bust me back to private. I had never wanted to be in command of anybody anyway, so the threat didn't mean much. What was he going to do? Send me to Vietnam and put me in the infantry? So what if I went to jail? I wouldn't be shot at again. Anyway, I was dismissed to do my job again.

Had I been more mature, I would have known that the best thing to do to help the platoon deal with their grief would have been to work their fannies off or put a rigorous training schedule in place. I didn't know that then, but I learned my lesson. Within the next couple of days, Staff Sgt. Campbell, our regular platoon sergeant, was back, and I was back with my squad. On December 26, 1967, I was promoted to staff sergeant E-6, with less than two years of service. My pay was $245.10 per month. I now outranked most of the men in my infantry company.

Just before New Year's Day 1968, the whole battalion was flown back to An Khe to pull Green Line duty. Alpha, Bravo, and Delta Companies were put on the perimeter of the fence surrounding Camp Radcliffe; we were put outside the wire to patrol and make sure the NVA or VC could not get close enough to mortar or snipe at Bob Hope's Christmas show. He had Raquel Welch with him.

One night after it was dark, we had just settled down for the night. I let the guys blow up their air mattresses, if they had one. We hardly ever let them do this because the mattresses made too much noise when they scooted around on them during the night. But we felt it was pretty safe that night. About eight o'clock, I heard a scream from one of our black guys who was lying in his makeshift hooch next to me.

I ran over to see what the matter was, and he blurted out, "Doug, there's something up my back and it's wiggling!"

I immediately unsnapped the ponchos that were serving as his tent and told him we were going to pull him up really fast and he should jump as high as he could and maybe the thing up his back would fall out. His eyes looked like silver dollars in the night. We pulled him up and as he jumped, a bamboo viper about two-and-a-half-feet long fell out of his fatigue jacket. The bamboo viper had crawled up his shirt while he was on his side, and when he turned over onto his back, it was trapped. The bamboo viper is called "old two-step." Loosely translated, it means that after you are bitten you take two steps, and you die. Someone killed it with a trenching tool and we all settled down again.

When we got back to Camp Radcliffe, I was walking by the area where Bob Hope had held his show. Painted on the outside of one of the latrines that had been built for them was, "Raquel Welch Shit Here!"

Sometime after the Bob Hope show, a few of my guys and I were put on duty in a sandbagged bunker on the back exit to Camp Radcliffe between Hong Cong Mountain and the Special Forces camp just west of An Khe. It was pretty boring duty.

One day with nothing to do, Dennis Rasmussen and I were talking about how fast I could draw a pistol. I borrowed someone's pistol and holster and soon we were outside the bunker facing each other down with holstered pistols. He went for his first, but I beat him and dry fired my pistol first. Dennis drew, cocked the hammer on his pistol, and it fired. The bullet went over my head. David Kipfinger, Dennis's assistant gunner, was behind me, and the bullet almost hit him. I stood mystified for a moment. Then rage that he had forgotten to unload his pistol welled up in me, and I started chasing him. I thought that if I caught him, I would teach him a lesson he would never forget. Fortunately, he outran me, and I eventually cooled down.

PART VI:
NORTH TO QUANG TRI

SEVEN AGAINST
SEVEN HUNDRED

Sometime in January 1968, we were called back into our rear support area where we were told we were going north to the DMZ. All we had ever heard and read about the DMZ was that this was where the Marines had encountered the heaviest fighting of the entire war. I met with our new captain, Capt. Bryant, and was told we would be flown up on C-130s. One of the last things I did in An Khe was let David Wilkowski stay behind. He was due to return to the States in February. He wanted to stay and pull KP in the rear as a short timer. I was sad to tell him good-bye. He promised to send me a bottle of bourbon in the mail after he returned to the States.

We began the journey in full field gear and backpacks. We got to the Hue/Phu Bai airstrip and loaded up on Hueys. We arrived at a newly formed LZ called Camp Evans. It was a mound of dirt perhaps three hundred by five hundred meters out in the middle of nowhere. The next day, they sent my squad out on a recon mission. We headed north toward a hill we could see in the distance. I didn't take a machine gun with me, but I did take a radio.

We got to the hill and ran into three North Vietnamese soldiers. We could see them about a hundred meters to our front.

The first thing I thought was that this was an ambush. I imagined they would run and lead us into a typical slaughter with deadly fire. I called back to our mortar platoon for a fire mission. I didn't ask for a hot round, but they sent a white phosphorus round that landed right in the middle of us. I thought I had given the correct coordinates, but it could have been my mistake or sometimes the maps are not exactly accurate. But I know I didn't call for a first round to be HE (high explosive) or WP (white phosphorus). I called off the fire mission and we cautiously walked further on with flanks out to check the area. The North Vietnamese were nowhere to be seen. When we returned back to the camp, I tried to find out who fired the white phosphorus round, but nobody would own up to the mistake.

After a couple of days, we were air assaulted out to a new LZ. I don't remember the name. We did a couple of patrols out of it, but there was no contact of any sort. One night someone had found some whiskey and beer and some of my guys were in a bunker drinking. I was with the platoon leader walking around checking all of our sleeping quarters and we walked in on them. Waskey was pretty drunk and in a sullen mood.

The lieutenant started in on them about being drunk, when Waskey drew a pistol on him and in slurred speech said, "You dirty son-of-a-bitch, you got Boeshart killed." The lieutenant turned white as a sheet.

He said in a very loud voice, "Waskey, put that pistol down or you'll be up for a court-martial." We were in the middle of a standoff.

My heart was down near my stomach, but I walked forward and began to talk to Waskey in a very low voice. I took the gun away from him and gave it to one of the guys. I quickly got the lieutenant out of there and talked to him at length about the advantage of not saying anything about what happened. I think I got my point across when I told him that if he turned Waskey in for a court-martial, someone else would be out for him. I promised I would talk with Waskey the next day and that it would never happen again. Waskey and I had a conversation the next day, and I told him I would shoot him myself if he ever pulled a stupid stunt like that again. I told the other guys to keep him away from the booze until he learned to control himself.

Our next assignment was to do a company sweep along Highway 1. The terrain was very much different from the Bong Son Plain. There were a lot of houses that looked like mansions to us. At times, we knocked on the doors of these houses to go inside and check them out. At one house, the door opened and a Vietnamese mother pushed her young daughter outside, as if offering her to us. I still to this day don't know what she did that for. For as long as we operated along Highway 1 until Tet, we didn't see a thing.

A couple of days later, we air assaulted from along Highway 1 to over near the Laotian border. We operated in company strength for a couple of days. We came upon a bombed out concrete bridge across a river and set up a perimeter to let most of the guys go swimming. A few of the guys used the opportunity to take a bath. That evening,

January 30th, I was assigned ambush for the night. My squad moved out about dusk. We couldn't see very far in front of us, because we were in high grass that came to our heads. Gouley heard some talking to our front, and we moved forward to see what was in front of us. About seven or eight North Vietnamese soldiers started firing at us. We returned fire, and they beat a hasty retreat. Since we were compromised, I asked permission via radio to come back in. The captain granted permission, and we came back into the perimeter for the night.

The next morning dawned bright and sunny. We were having breakfast when we received a call to find a place to be air assaulted out. We slung our backpacks together into a net sling for Chinooks to come and pick up. I didn't know it then, but it would be several days before we would see our packs again. The operations order said we would be going to Quang Tri and swinging south along Highway 1 to begin a sweep south of the city. My squad was on the first Huey in the air assault formation. I had my entire squad of seven guys, including me. We had a radio, but not a single machine gun with us. One of the machine gun crews was behind us with the platoon leader on the second chopper. The terrain below us was absolutely beautiful. I slid out of my seat and stood on the right strut of the helicopter.

I looked out along Highway 1 and could see a column of soldiers on either side of the highway. As we approached, I saw them hitting the dirt. It was then I realized these guys were wearing khakis and they were North Vietnamese out in the open in broad daylight. We were about fifteen feet off the highway when the Plexiglas windshield shattered. One of the pilots looked back and motioned for me to get out of the helicopter. All of us jumped out onto Highway

1 and immediately took off for the rice paddy dike that ran alongside the highway.

We had been dropped into the middle of an NVA Regiment on the march. Just behind them were NVA artillery units that had come into South Vietnam to provide fire support for the taking of Quang Tri.

Here we were, out in the middle of a rice paddy, along the side of the highway, stranded. Billy Cabaniss had the radio, and Morgan, Gouley, Osborne, Richards, and Nibbelink were with me but the rest of the company was not in sight. The rest of the air assault had been aborted and the helicopters flew away and left us. The ARA helicopters that had accompanied our main force began to fire on the soldiers in front us. We watched on our backs as one of the ARA helicopters was shot down. It crashed and burned about five hundred meters from us. There was no evidence of any survivors. There was nothing we could do. It would have been suicide to cover five hundred meters in the withering fire we were drawing. We were behind a rice paddy dike in the worst mud I have ever been in. Buster Morgan had been shot in the thumb and was bleeding pretty bad. He had wrapped a bandage around it and was continuing to function. Every once in a while, one of us would put our rifle over the dike and spray bullets out in front us, just to let the NVA know we were still capable of fighting.

I don't know how long we were out there. We watched as gunships with ARA and mini-guns made run after run over the enemy positions in front of us. Then we heard jets and F-4s begin to drop napalm bombs on the enemy out to our front. The fire finally abated enough for Col. French to land his helicopter near us. He could only take half of us, so I sent three of my guys with him and he came back about 20 minutes later for the rest of us. We scrambled aboard and began the flight to an LZ near Quang Tri and out of harm's way. This battle was the start of Tet for us. The Tet Offensive of 1968 caught our leadership unaware of the massive NVA troop buildup around the major cities in South Vietnam.

The rest of the company was engaged in a fight, though I do not how far they were from us. They lost two men, Spec. 4th Class Harold Cashman, Jr., and Cpl. Damon Ritchie. One of the wounded that day was Tom Corey. His wounds made him a paraplegic. Rich Valles and John Spencer crawled out to get Corey under heavy fire. They drug him back behind a rice paddy dike and Valles used mouth-to-mouth resuscitation to get him breathing again. Spencer kept firing at the enemy to keep their heads down while Valles was trying to save Corey's life. Corey started breathing again, but then started fading in and out of consciousness. Valles thought he was dying, so he tried to keep him awake. He started calling Corey's wife all sorts of bad names to try and get Corey mad. When Corey again faded into unconsciousness, he punched him a couple of times in the ribs. Valles, a former Golden Gloves boxer, underestimated his strength. After Corey made it to a hospital, he and his doctors were puzzled about his wounds. They could explain the neck wound that left him paralyzed, but were unable to explain why he had three cracked ribs.

John Spencer was hard to get to know. He didn't drink alcohol, didn't curse and never went down town with us when we were on stand-down. He wore glasses and was really an intellectual. He quoted poems and classical writers. But, he was a good soldier, just putting in his time to go home and resume his civilian life.

All in all, I remember that for sixteen straight days after Tet began, we were in contact. By that, I mean we drew and returned fire. We got into one heck of a firefight on one of those days. We were spread out as a company, sweeping through the terrain around a village when we received heavy small arms fire and mortars. I remember seeing two or three of our guys who were behind a huge tree in the middle of a rice paddy. A mortar round hit right behind them and they moved to the front of the tree. Then a mortar round hit in front of the tree and they moved back to their original position. That was the day the guy I kept from marrying the Vietnamese prostitute found a dead NVA officer with a pistol and pistol belt on him. He put it inside his fatigue jacket and kept it as a souvenir. We lost three guys in this battle. They were Spec. 4th Class Larry Clark, Pfc. John Dashnaw, and Pfc. John Kuiper.

One night after drawing small arms fire all day, we set up to form a company perimeter. Billy Cabaniss went outside the perimeter to set up a claymore mine. While he was kneeling down inserting the claymore into the ground, he felt a tap on his shoulder and looked up to see two NVA soldiers. They began talking to him in Vietnamese. Evidently, in the dark they thought he was one of them. Cabaniss had not brought his weapon with him. He was only fifteen or twenty feet outside our position. The only thing he could think of to do was to throw a cross body block, a football maneuver, on them. He hit them as hard as he could and then ran back into our perimeter. He dove into our foxhole, breathing hard. When he explained what happened, several of the guys and I went out to where he had been, but could find no one. He must have scared them as bad as they scared him.

Another day just before dusk, I went outside our perimeter and set up an automatic ambush—a grenade rigged to go off instantly when the trip wire was tripped. I had had a feeling all day that we had been followed. That night, the captain was sending out an ambush team on a route that would take them directly into the path of my automatic ambush. So, without a flashlight, I had to crawl out to where I had set the grenade, grab the handle in the dark, re-inset the pin and take it down. I took my time and got it done.

KILLER TEAM

It was about this time I got a new platoon leader, 2nd Lt. Dave Carmody. He was as green as a gourd. He had been through officer candidate school and airborne training. I remember thinking at the time that I was glad he had been to jump school. At least he would know how to handle fear. I took it upon myself to teach him everything I could. I was very rude to him at times.

I should have toned down my speeches to him. I would explain how we should walk when we were on patrol and how to handle the men. I tried to give him the rundown on those men he could count on to do a good job and those whom he would have to keep an eye on. I told him what I considered important and what was immaterial. I was careful not to give him advice in front of the men. I would take him aside and tell him why his ideas were less than adequate and what I would have said in place of what he had said to the men. He was receptive and thanked me several times for the advice, but I kept thinking he might be resentful. I was grateful that I was able to train him in what I considered the right way to do things. I heard he became a very capable platoon leader before his six months in the field were up.

One morning a week or two after Tet, we slung our packs out for the helicopters to pick up, only to see it cloud up and rain. We patrolled all day in a company formation with my squad walking point. That night we were picked to go out on a "killer team." I wasn't too happy about it, since we had been on point all day. But without packs and poncho liners, I knew everybody was going to be miserable anyway, so I accepted my assignment without much talk.

The killer team concept was thought up by some officer on staff somewhere. The idea was to send six guys out no more than one kilometer to patrol all night. If and when they came into contact with the enemy, the rest of the company was to join them to engage the enemy. So, I picked five guys to go with me, including Jerry Richards, Phillip Hayes and Billy Cabaniss. It was a cloudy night with no moon. I took my squad about a hundred meters outside the perimeter to a trail, and we all squatted to let me get a look at the trail before we proceeded.

At night when there is no moon, we would lie down on the ground and, rather than look directly at what we were trying to see, we'd look at it from an angle. If we stared long enough, this method gave us a better sense of the landscape, trees, and other cover that might provide protection for the enemy. The army called this night vision. As I looked east down the trail, I could see five to seven people walking down the trail. About one hundred yards behind them, there was another column of people walking down the trail. I quickly whispered to my team that I had seen movement. With hand signals, I indicated there were at least five people coming toward us. I also indicated to switch off the safety on their weapons.

When the first column of what turned out to be six people got to within ten meters of us, I opened up with my M-16. The rest of the guys followed suit. It was so dark we couldn't see what we hit. Just then, the column behind them opened up on us; we got low so we wouldn't get hit. While this was going on, I got on the radio Billy was carrying and called back for illumination rounds. When the first flare exploded over our heads, we could see three bodies lying in front of us. By this time, Cliff Metz had joined us with his machine gun crew, so I left him to gather the equipment while we started out after the enemy that got away.

We ran about a hundred meters to a rice paddy and found the other three from the first column. They continued firing at us. The guys shot two of them, and as I stepped over a dike. The third enemy soldier rose up from behind the dike and drew a bead either on my back or Cabaniss. Hayes was behind us and shot him with an M-79 round. He was close to the enemy soldier, but not close enough to prevent the grenade from exploding. Some of the shrapnel hit Cabaniss.

To get the artillery guys to continue to illuminate the surroundings, we had to promise to give them credit for all the kills we made; otherwise, they didn't want to use all of their illumination rounds in support of our operations. It had something to do with the numbers game everyone played to be able to ask for more ammunition.

But soon the firing stopped and it was pitch black again. We walked back to where Cliff Metz and his gun crew were and got all the packs and weapons. We also recovered a 61 mm mortar tube and the base plate. We took all the stuff back to our company commander. Since we were compromised, we didn't have to go back out. We found some rainproof liners in the enemy backpacks, which we slept in the rest of the night. I joked to Capt. Bryant that since we couldn't get our packs back out in the rainy weather, I had been forced to go out and find my own rain gear. The Cavalair ran an article about this incident, and I've reprinted it here.

Six On Six But Cavalry Alter Odds

QUANG TRI—Six 1st Air Cavalrymen ran into six North Vietnamese Army Regulars in the stillness of night and cut three of them down during the battle for this city much of which was fought in the suburbs.

The men were a killer team dispatched by Charlie Company of the 1st Air Cavalry Division's 1st Battalion, 12th Cavalry who were assigned to shoot any enemy they found.

The team's leader, Staff Sergeant Douglas Warden said, "We saw them skylined on the bank of a narrow river . . . we got on our bellies and let them have it."

Three went down and the others fled.

The First Brigade killer team crossed a nearby bridge and approached the downed enemy.

Two were dead, but another raised his rifle at Specialist Four Billy Cabbannis as he neared. Cabannis stopped him with a burst from his rifle before the enemy was able to squeeze off a round.

The article didn't get it exactly right, because Hayes had been the one to kill the soldier drawing a bead on me and Cabaniss, but it was mostly correct.

The next day, the first sergeant took me to Capt. Bryant. They told me they wanted to submit my name and records to the West Point Preparatory School. They said this would prepare me for West Point. I know they were sincere, but at the time, I just wasn't interested.

"I've only got two years in this man's army, and then I'm out. Nobody could talk me into staying in!" It is one of the dumbest decisions I have ever made. I don't regret much about the decisions I've made in life, but this one I've really regretted through the years. This would have been a way to finish college on the army's nickel, and I blew it.

During the sixteen days that we were in constant contact, my squad was put on point almost every time we moved out in company formation. I knew this was supposed to be an honor, but it was getting a little ridiculous. One day we moved out and hadn't moved over a click when we came up against significant small arms fire. It seemed to be coming from a house to our front. My squad used advance and covering fire to get up close to the house. I yelled out, "Choi hoi! Choi hoi!"—which means in Vietnamese to give up or surrender.

There was not a sound from the house, so I pulled the pin on a grenade and heaved it in a window. After the explosion, we heard screaming and crying. We rushed inside to find a Vietnamese man in orange robes (probably a Buddhist priest), a woman I assumed was his wife and several children. The priest was dead; his wife and children were wounded. We called for a medevac to get the wife and children to a hospital.

About thirty minutes later, after we got the wounded on the helicopter, a South Vietnamese NCO rode up on a motor scooter. We were surprised to see him, because we never saw a South Vietnamese soldier out by himself on a scooter coming to investigate a firefight. He went into the house where I had thrown the grenade. Evidently, the priest was related to him. Somehow, he procured a coffin for the priest's body and wanted us to help him carry it back to the road. I didn't want to help him, because I figured that before long he would find out I was the one who had thrown the grenade that killed his relative. But my guilt got the better of me, and I asked a few of the guys, including Charles Fletcher, to help me with the coffin. We got it to the road and then went back to join the rest of the company.

It was at this time that I noticed a black guy who had joined our unit. If I remember correctly, his name was John Myers. He was a private E-1, but on his fatigue hat he wore jump wings with the airborne black and green oval background of the 12th Cavalry.

I asked him, "Who are you, and why are you wearing the airborne background for the 1st Battalion?" His answer was that he had gone over with Charlie Company in 1965 and had gone AWOL while on leave to Hawaii. He had evaded arrest, but eventually gave himself up. His choice was either to go to the stockade for being AWOL in a combat zone or return to Charlie Company as a private E-1 and serve out his time. He chose the latter. Here he was as an enlisted man in the 1st of the 12th, still drawing jump pay. It was over five months since the last of the airborne guys left for other airborne assignments, and we still had a few with us who continued to draw jump pay. Jerome "Doc" Bacon, of HHQ Company, was back in Quang Tri drawing jump pay. Doc Bacon, who had received the Silver Star for the Battle of Hoa Hoi in October 1966, had extended and had been grandfathered to still draw his parachute pay.

My squad was picked to go out on another killer team later that week. I took five guys with me. One of the guys who accompanied me was Jerry Richards of Ohio. We moved about one thousand meters to the north and east of our perimeter and came upon a village. I decided to set up an ambush just outside the village. We set out trip flares all around us and across a trail that went into the village. We were in some kind of a vegetable garden, lying prone on the ground.

We hadn't been set up very long before we began to hear movement to our front. We all switched on full automatic with our rifles and waited. One trip flare began burning white-hot. A small herd of deer had tripped the flare and they were scurrying like crazy in circles as they set off one trip flare after another. When I say small deer, I mean I had never seen anything like them. They stood a foot to a foot and a half tall. These small deer were a miniature deer species I had never heard of. To say they scared us is an understatement.

THIRD PURPLE HEART

On February 19th, we came up against a numerically superior NVA force just south and east of Quang Tri. The fire went hot and heavy for a while. Sgt. John Madison, one of Metz's friends from another platoon, was killed that day. He was hit by an RPG that took off his head. I was platoon sergeant that day and spent most of my time directing the fire of our machine guns toward the enemy positions. They were dug in, in long trenches in front of us. At some point, we realized there was CS gas—tear gas—in the air. Those of us who had gas masks quickly put them on.

I was lying down facing toward the enemy positions when I felt something like a bee sting on my right hip. I slapped at it, thinking it was an insect. When I looked at my hand, it had blood on it. A gunshot wound to my hip had just barely creased my skin. I've joked through the years that I was shot in the back while facing the enemy, but actually, we got hit from the rear. I don't know how the round missed my head and hit me in the hip.

After the contact subsided, we found out the helicopters couldn't fly because it was too cloudy and foggy. That meant we'd have to get through the night without our backpacks, chow or medical care. We formed a company perimeter in wet sand. I had a poncho on my web belt, so; Cliff Metz and I lay down and rolled up in it for the night. It got cold, so we would take turns lighting our cigarette lighters to get warm enough to get back to sleep. That went on all night, until we finally ran out of cigarette lighter fluid and we shivered the rest of the night. My hip wound bled all night long. I resolved to get out the next morning to the hospital.

When the choppers arrived the next morning, I went back to the rear to see about my hip wound. The doctor at the forward rear area in Quang Tri put a black butterfly suture over the wound to seal it shut, but it was infected so he ordered me to stay in the rear for three to four weeks. That would put me close to my time to go home. I walked over to the Charlie Company forward rear area and told the guys I was there to stay. That was my third Purple Heart. The rule was that guys were taken out of the field with two. I assumed this applied only to enlisted men, because I was an NCO, and they kept me in the field after my second Purple Heart. Now I had two reasons to stay in the rear. I was under medical care and had my third Purple Heart.

I became the NCOIC of the forward rear area. This was the job I was supposed to have been assigned to when I returned from R&R back in November. The NCOIC's job in the rear area was to receive nightly radio transmissions from the field concerning ammo and equipment resupply, gather everything the next day and make sure it went out on the chow chopper in the afternoon.

Cliff Metz told me later that several of the guys complained about me not coming back to the field and accused me of being a coward. He stood up for me and told them I had been in the field for ten months and hadn't missed one round being fired at the company. Cliff said that seemed to put a stop to the complaining.

As for me, I missed the guys, but I was homesick and had no thoughts of staying in the army. I just wanted to get out when my time came and I didn't care what anyone thought. After I left the company to go to work in the rear, they went into the A Shau Valley and participated in the operation to do clean-up operations around Khe San.

PART VII:
IN THE REAR

CLOSE CALL

Several days after I was back in the rear, one of the guys from my old platoon came back on the returning chow chopper. He came to me, crying. He told me he had received a "Dear John" letter. His girlfriend or wife, I don't remember which, was leaving him. I took him to the chaplain who got him a thirty-day emergency leave to return to the States. After about ten days, he was back in Quang Tri. When I asked him why he was back so soon, he told me one of the most outlandish stories I believe I have ever heard. He said when he returned to his home in the States, he didn't phone anyone, not even his parents.

He took a cab to a store and bought a pair of nylon hose and a baseball bat. He then went to his girl's home and waited in the bushes. When his girl returned home with her newfound male companion, he came out of the bushes wearing the nylon hose on his head and wielding a baseball bat. He beat them both until they stopped moving but made sure they both were still alive. Then he took off the hose, dropped the bat near them and went back out to the airport to catch the next flight out to California to return to Vietnam. No one ever knew he was home.

While in the rear, I was bunking with a guy from the 3rd platoon who had received two Purple Hearts and had come out of the field. We had a small circular tent surrounded by sandbags. My bunkmate was Duane McAndrews from Nebraska. He was one of the guys who had gone downtown in Bong Son after our battle on December 15 and16 and gotten into trouble. McAndrews, a licensed barber back in the States, became the barber for the entire battalion and kept busy all day, every day. Billy Cabaniss came by on his way back out to the field, looking for McAndrews and a haircut. As a joke, I told him Mac had been giving me lessons, so he let me cut his hair. I screwed it up so badly, that Mac had to give him a burr haircut to fix it. It was such a shame. Cabaniss had long, blond hair. He was really mad at me.

McAndrews stole a jeep out of the motor pool and asked me if I wanted to go to downtown Quang Tri to the NCO club at the Navy compound. Because both Mac and I were NCOs, we waltzed right in and started drinking. On the way back, Mac rear-ended a man riding a bicycle. The man was not hurt, but Mac stopped the truck and threw the bike in the bar ditch beside the road. He got the jeep back in the motor pool without getting caught.

I was beginning to get used to running the rear forward area, when Capt. Bentson showed up one day in March. He had some kind of business in Quang Tri. He took me aside and asked me if I would like to come back to An Khe and work for him. I jumped at the chance. He said he would speak with Col. French. After their conversation, Col. French asked for me to come by his quarters to talk with him.

That night after dark, I made my way to Col. French's quarters, which were underground. The roof, at ground level, was made with the interlocking metal planks used to construct runways and was covered with sandbags. I misjudged the first step, and I fell down the stairs and through the poncho covering the entrance. Col. French was at a desk and looked up at me lying on his floor.

He quipped, "Sgt. Warden, nice of you to drop in!" I had to laugh at his making a joke at my expense. We talked for a while and he told me it was okay to transfer to the 15th Admin Company, which Capt. Bentson commanded.

The next day, Capt. Bentson, a sergeant first class whose name I don't remember, and I boarded a C-130 for the first leg of our flight back to An Khe. It was cloudy, so as we approached the Hue/Phu Bai airstrip, we had to circle lower and lower until we could come out of the cloud cover and land. Just as we came out of the clouds and could see the landscape below, I heard several rattling sounds coming from inside our aircraft. We had been hit by small arms fire and the rounds had penetrated the bottom of the aircraft, but didn't have enough velocity to exit through the roof, so they just rattled around inside. No one was hurt by the rounds. The air force crew scrambled around checking things out. They found that the hydraulics had been knocked out by the rounds.

We were immediately rerouted to Da Nang to land. The crew used a manual crank to turn the wheels to landing position. They couldn't quite get the gears all the way down and locked. We circled the airfield for quite a long time. The pilot was trying to burn off the excess fuel, in case the landing gear wouldn't hold and we belly-landed. I began to think a lot about my life while we were circling.

The first thing I thought was that I had so many close calls in the field, and now I was going to die in a plane crash. Before long, the crew chief told us to pick up our legs just before touchdown. We landed on the Da Nang runway and began our slowdown. About two hundred meters down the runway, the gears gave way, and the belly of the aircraft hit the pavement. Fortunately, the ground crew had foamed the runway. When we finally stopped at the end of the runway, we got off the airplane as quickly as we could.

We went inside the terminal and found out the next plane to An Khe wasn't leaving until the next day. There were a couple of guys waiting on a plane wearing green berets, the headgear for Special Forces. Capt. Bentson had spent some time with Special Forces at Fort Bragg, NC, before his deployment to Vietnam, so he struck up a conversation with one of them, a white-haired first lieutenant named Todd.

Lt. Todd told Bentson that Da Nang was the headquarters for Special Forces team C-1, and mentioned a few names that Bentson knew who were there. We caught a ride to C-1, and Capt. Bentson did indeed know people there. We were fed and given sleeping quarters for the night. The next day, we trucked back to the airport at Da Nang and caught a plane out to An Khe.

CHARM SCHOOL CADRE

When we got to An Khe, Capt. Bentson put me in charge of the daily latrine burning detail. They had some slackers who were always in trouble, and it was up to me to get them up, dressed, and out for formation every day. Their job was to pull out the shortened barrels filled with waste material from underneath the latrines. Then they would mix in diesel and set the mixture on fire. After about an hour or two, everything would be gone from the barrels, and they were to re-insert them under the latrines.

I had trouble getting these guys up the first day, but not the second. I walked into their sleeping quarters the second day and shook the first guy awake. I pulled the pin from a grenade and handed it to him as he lay there. I told him that all of them had ten seconds to get outside and hand it back to me, so I could replace the pin. What they didn't know was that I had removed the firing device inside the grenade. I waited for them as they barreled outside for formation in their underwear. I took the grenade and put the pin back in. I told them if they were ever late again, I would just throw it in their sleeping quarters. Word got around that I was crazy, and I never had trouble with them again.

Day after day, I was through with work by noon. I would check out a jeep and go to the Charlie Company rear area and visit with the guys in the rear. Sometimes the guys from the field would come over to the 15th Admin company area when they were going on R&R or coming back from the hospital, and I would take them by Capt. Bentson's quarters to see him. One night, Phillip Hayes and Calvin Gouley came by to see me. I took them to Capt. Bentson's hooch and we had several drinks. Before the night was over, Capt. Bentson swept his forearm across the table to clear all the glasses and bottles and then arm wrestled with Hayes. I don't remember who won, but we had a great time. I know Bentson really enjoyed seeing some of the guys from the field. He was surrounded by rear echelon guys and found it refreshing to spend time with some of the infantrymen he had commanded in November and December 1967.

I attended a cookout and drinking session one night at Bentson's invitation. At one point he was talking with an NCO who was in charge of the various club operations at An Khe. Their conversation grew heated, and before I knew it, he slapped the sergeant first class. The sergeant looked at me and asked if I had witnessed the altercation. I told him I hadn't seen a thing. After Bentson left, I went over to the NCO and, in a very low voice, told him that if he tried to bring Bentson up on charges, I would put him in the hospital. His face turned white as a sheet. I meant it, and he knew it. The guy had been dealing PX goods to the black market. He was one of the reasons guys in the field had such a shortage of clothing and equipment. I don't know what happened to him, but I hope he went to jail.

Capt. Bentson put me in charge of replacing the big Cav patch displayed on Hong Kong Mountain. Some guys from the 173rd Airborne had driven a jeep up to the top and attempted to paint their own patch over the 1st Cav patch that had been there for several years. I had the guys in the motor pool paint a huge patch on a piece of rubber-like material that was used under the PSP railing for a metal runway. When it was done, Capt. Bentson and I, along with about fifteen others, went up on the mountain, attached the sheet of rubber to an anchor board, and let it unfurl down the side of the mountain. It took us about two hours to hang the new patch.

I was finally given a respectable job just before I left. I became an instructor for the orientation classes for the new recruits just coming in country. I liked that a lot better. I gave a class on infantry tactics and took the men outside the wire for their one night of bivouac.

I remember one night being in the NCO club drinking with someone who also had been in the field. We heard the distinctive whistle-boom of a mortar attack and watched the rear echelon guys hit the floor. We sat there and continued drinking because, from the sound of the exploding rounds, we knew they weren't even close to us.

Another night in the club, I ran into a guy who cut orders for soldiers to return to the United States. He told me that for a bottle of his favorite liquor, he would get me home two weeks early. I jumped at the chance. The next day I took him a bottle of whatever it was he wanted. On April 30th, I boarded a plane to go to Cam Ranh Bay for departure to the States a full two weeks before I was supposed to go back. There was a machine gunner from the 1st platoon who was on the same plane with me. I think his name was Williams. He was a good guy. We out-processed that day and were scheduled to fly out the next morning. That night at the Enlisted Men's Club, we were having drinks in our class-A khakis. At our table was Williams and Staff Sgt. Hazelip's tank driver from the first major battle I was in on May 31st.

There was another guy at the table who accused me of buying my stripes and all my ribbons at the PX. He thought I looked much too young to be a staff sergeant with ten medals on my uniform, some with oak leaf clusters on them. I started to stand up and take him on when the tank driver restrained me and told me it wasn't worth it. A bigger concern was hearing that someone had packed two fragmentation grenades in his duffle bag. I didn't want to cause a stink and especially didn't want to hold up the departure of the plane the next morning, so I kept my mouth shut and just prayed that he had crimped the ends of the pins that held the handles on.

PART VIII:
AFTER VIETNAM

GOING HOME

I don't remember much about the flight home. I know we landed in Japan and then Alaska. Finally, we landed in Seattle, WA. The next thing I knew we were on a bus to Ft. Lewis. I was there for my discharge papers and a flight home. While I was out-processing, the colonel in charge sent for me. He told me I was the most decorated draftee he had seen come through Ft. Lewis. He said he was going to send his sergeant first class recruiter to talk with me about staying in. I politely told him there was no way I would stay in. I just wanted to go home. It wasn't too long before I had all the pay due to me and my discharge, along with a brand new uniform to wear home.

Williams was from Oregon, and he was also getting out. We caught a taxi together to the airport. Our taxi driver was a soldier who moonlighted as a driver. We offered to buy him a drink at the airport, so he came in with us. Later we went to the USO to get a bunk for the night. The next morning a lady from the USO woke me up for my flight home.

I boarded a flight to Tulsa not knowing I had a second ticket to Oklahoma City in the ticket jacket. I got to Tulsa and thought I was stranded there because someone had made a mistake. I had thrown away the other ticket.

I took a taxi downtown and bought some jeans, a shirt, and shoes to wear. I got back out to the airport and I heard my name over the paging system. Aunt Betty, my mom's sister, was on the line. She asked me why I wasn't on the flight from Tulsa to Oklahoma City. When I explained to her that I didn't know about the other ticket, she bought me a ticket to catch the next flight. When I arrived in Oklahoma City, there was my mom, Aunt Betty, my mother's brother, Uncle Bob, and his son, Stan.

Mom was just beside herself, and Betty kept telling her, "See Katherene, he's all right!" Mom asked me if I wanted to drive, and I told her I would try. I had not driven over thirty mph in over a year, so I drove at thirty mph for over thirty miles to Mom and Dad's farm.

When we drove up the driveway to our house, my dad was there, on his way out to the barn to do the chores. He shook my hand and told me he was glad I was home. He wasn't half as glad as I was.

REFLECTIONS

After I was discharged, I returned to my old job at Tinker Air Force Base. My wife, Marty, and I married in August 1968, and after nine months of marriage, she became pregnant with our first child.

I didn't like the job I had at Tinker, so I applied to the Oklahoma City Police Department and went through the screening and testing process. I was accepted, but I had to turn them down when I found out maternity benefits didn't kick in until an employee had been on the job nine months. The anticipated cost to have a child at that time was six hundred dollars. It might as well have been ten thousand dollars. I couldn't afford for us to have a child without medical insurance.

I was very dissatisfied with my job, so when I attended the Oklahoma State Fair in October 1969, I visited the tent for US Army enlistments. I told them I would go back in, if I could keep my E-6 stripes. They told me a new rule had just come out that gave a departing soldier up to thirty months to re-enlist and keep his former rank. When I heard that, I was ready to go back in. I waited almost a year at Ft. Devens, MA, for my top secret and crypto clearance to come through to begin school at the US Army Security

Agency. I ended up volunteering to go back on jump status to join one of the ASA detachments that were integrated into each Special Forces Group.

I put in about three and a half more years in the military until I had an accident while serving with the 1st Special Forces Group (Airborne) on Okinawa, Japan. I made a "Hollywood" exit from a thirty-four-foot parachute tower on July 18, 1972, snapping the 9/16-inch cable that was supposed to keep me suspended. I fell onto the hard ground, crushing my right wrist, injuring my back, and cracking several of my teeth. The cable whipped back and would have decapitated the men, who were unsnapping us as we rode down, had they not ducked down behind a mound of dirt.

I was medically retired and returned to college on the GI Bill, graduating with a BA in management in 1980.

When the World Trade Center came down on September 11, 2001, I would have re-enlisted. I would have wanted to be in a combat arms branch of the army, so I could get up close and personal with the enemy. But, as Clint Eastwood has said in his movies, "Every man has to know his limitations." I was too old and slow to do that kind of thing anymore.

Here's where every author who writes about Vietnam gets to tell his opinions about the Vietnam War effort. First of all, I would do it again in a heartbeat. If I had Vietnam to do over, I would try to grow up a little quicker and not do so many dumb things. I would also limit my alcohol intake. But I tried to do the best I could with my limited experience.

I don't think the military lost the war in Vietnam; our government gave it away. I never heard of any battles we lost. We won all the battles, but lost the war. We lost because of the negative US press. We lost because of the rotation policy for our troops. I think it's pretty stupid to bring troops home after just a year's tour of duty in wartime. We were robbed of valuable experience in our NCO and officer corps. We also came out on the short end of the stick because the war was being run in a political manner. President Johnson had no business trying to run the war from the White House. And finally, I think the American people gave up on the war effort. Americans don't support anything for very long. We are fickle people. They just lost interest in winning. The press told them that we weren't winning, and they wanted us to get out.

I wish I could say I've never had a bad dream or that Vietnam hasn't affected me in any way, but that's not true. Vietnam has changed me in several ways. I stopped hunting after Vietnam. I just didn't want to handle guns or rifles after that year. I never really got excited or upset about anything after Vietnam. I just always thought to myself, "*Well, they aren't shooting real bullets.*" That seemed to put everything in perspective.

I sometimes dream about carrying Rick Boeshart on my back as I run toward a medevac helicopter. Sometimes the helicopter takes off before I can get there. Never in my dreams am I able to keep him alive. I also dream sometimes that I'm standing in one of the mock airplane doors on a thirty-four-foot parachute tower, like the one I was on when I got hurt on Okinawa in 1972. I am standing there, and I'm trying to decide whether to ask the instructor if I can be excused from jumping out of the tower. Or, I'm in a quandary to decide to go ahead and jump. I also wake up frequently at night, thinking immediately when I open my eyes that I've gone to sleep on guard. It's been a long time since I've had a good night's sleep.

I learned a lot about managing people in Vietnam. I'll give you three things I did leading men in combat that carried over to my private life and management style. The first thing is that you have to lead from the front. You lead by example rather than by command. I learned leading by example commands respect, rather than demands respect. In Vietnam, I assumed no one knew what to do better than me. Every manager needs to lead and not manage. That's difficult to do in a top down organization.

The second thing is that you cannot affect everything. I wrote down everything I could and would change, and I wrote down everything I couldn't change. I only worked on those things I could change for the better.

And, lastly, you have to help people improve. I always tried to assess every man and look at his strengths and his weaknesses. I praised and complimented their strengths, and I gave suggestions for making them better as individual soldiers. I found that addressing their weaknesses with improvement plans made the group better as a whole. It takes more time to do things that way, but it is more effective.

Trying to do more than this makes you less effective. Putting everything you have into accomplishing those three things every day will take you far in any organization.

I have also changed my relationship with God. I now know that being a Christian is being in a state of grace. During Vietnam, I thought if I died with a sin attributed to me, I would be lost. I'm much more comfortable with my faith now.

After I returned home, I became very close to my parents. It's a shame that boys take so long to grow up and really appreciate their parents and what they do for them. I'm satisfied that my parents knew how much I loved them before they died. I also have no regrets about how I treated them and the way I tried to take care of them in their old age.

I find I have very few friends who live close to me. My old friends from high school and childhood are still my friends, but I'm not as close to them as I am the guys I was with in Vietnam. The bond is such that I could get a call from any number of them, and I would do anything for them. It's nice to know guys who would give their life for you. As I near the end of my life, I have a lot of peace knowing I have known some of the finest and bravest men who have ever walked this earth and that I have their respect. I hope they know they have mine. I believe this quote from an unknown author says it all about how I feel:

> "I now know why men who have been to war yearn to reunite. Not to tell stories or look at old pictures. Not to laugh or weep. Comrades gather because they long to be with the men who once acted at their best; men who suffered and sacrificed, who suffered and were stripped of their humanity.
>
> "I did not pick these men. They were delivered by fate and the military. But I know them in a way I know no other men. I have never given anyone such trust. They were willing to guard something more precious than my life. They would have carried my

reputation to the end, the memory of me. It was part of the bargain we all made, the reason we were so willing to die for one another. As long as I have memory, I will think of them all, every day. I am sure that when I leave this world, my last thought will be of my family and my comrades ... such good men!"

EPILOGUE

About a month after my wife and I were married, we returned home to find *Cliff Metz* sitting in a car outside our apartment. He had driven to Oklahoma from Ft. Hood, Texas, with an army buddy of his to see me. We have kept in touch through the years. He is a sub-contractor in Ohio and has raised four kids as a single parent. He was a terrific machine gunner and soldier

Tom Cusick and his first wife drove to Oklahoma from Lees Summit, MO, in August 1969. My wife and I were observing our first wedding anniversary. Tom and his wife were going to take us out to celebrate. They proceeded to have the biggest fight I've ever witnessed a married couple have. The episode ruined our anniversary. He and his wife later divorced. His wife fought him constantly about seeing their daughters. He had limited contact with them until they were old enough to be on their own. I kept in touch with him and his second wife through the years. He came to Dallas when I was living there and stayed with me for several days. He died of cancer in 1994. I visited him in the hospital in Kansas City before he died, and I attended his funeral service in Missouri. He was a good friend to me.

Larry Ashley did survive his wounds caused by the booby trap explosion in June of 1967. He lost both of his legs. Charles Church, our former company clerk, helped me to find him. Charles remembered Ashley mentioning his first wife's name. We googled the name and found out that his first wife was buried near where he lived in Northeast Texas. I got his phone number and Charles Fletcher and I drove down to see him. He was in an army hospital for nine months and then discharged. The VA hospital kept him for nine months and fitted him for prosthetic legs. Three weeks after his discharge from the hospital, he was back at work for a Texas high tech company, where he retired some thirty years later. He is now an elected official in Northeast Texas, has remarried, and has a great attitude toward life. I was so glad to find him whole, both in body and in spirit.

Phillip Hayes drove his new Dodge Charger to my folks' farm and stayed with me a couple of days after we got home in 1968. He returned to Chelsea, OK, bought a farm, got married, and had two daughters. He and his brother were killed when they moved a grain auger into a bare electric wire near his barn. I didn't even know when he was killed. Losing Hayes caused me some grief. I blame myself for no one in his family knowing we were close friends and notifying me about his death. I resolved that after that I would make sure nothing like that would happen again. I've visited his grave outside of Chelsea.

Maj. Peter M. Bentson, our former company commander in Charlie Company, was killed on board a hovering helicopter during an artillery attack in Vietnam in early July 1972. He was an advisor and general's aide to a Vietnamese army unit. I read about his death in the *Stars and Stripes* newspaper. He had three kids. He would have been chief of staff of the army had he lived. He was one fine officer and man.

Charles Fletcher, my fellow Okie, still lives in Oklahoma City. He was an air conditioning repairman and has several kids and grandkids. He is now retired. His daughter graduated from law school in Ohio. He was able to see and talk with Cliff Metz when he was in Ohio for her graduation.

Bob Radcliffe, my platoon leader, stayed in the Army for twenty-six years, retiring as a full bird colonel. He was an advisor to the Iranian Special Forces, had a tour with the 46th Special Forces in Thailand, went through an advanced course for armor at Ft. Knox, completed his master's degree in Georgia, and became a battalion commander and assistant brigade commander of the 6th Recruiting District. He finished his career as the inspector general of the Army Recruiting Command. He became a senior manager for Phillip Morris in civilian life. He is now retired. I talk to him at least once a month. He invites me to his West Point class of 1965 golf outings twice a year. I'm the only former enlisted man who attends these golf outings. They are a fine bunch of men whom I admire very much. Bob credits me with saving his life by pulling him back before he stepped on a booby trap, though whether I did or not is questionable. He has been a great friend to me through the years. We have taken golf trips, fishing trips in Mexico, and shared many memories.

Buster Morgan has never responded to any of my letters. I talked to his brother in Texas at one point. He told me Buster lives and works just outside of town and doesn't even have a telephone. Evidently, he doesn't even want to think about Vietnam. He was one of the best men I had in the platoon.

Earl Osborne re-enlisted in the army for a while after Vietnam. He was stationed in Germany and became the army boxing champ of Europe for his weight class. He got out and returned to North Carolina, where he still lives. I've seen him three or four times since Vietnam. He credits me with keeping him alive during Vietnam. I believe he would do almost anything within his power for me. He has been a great friend.

David Wilkowski lives in Michigan. He does construction work and is off every winter. This last September, David and his wife drove down from Michigan to Branson, Missouri to see me. David and I belong to a mutual admiration club. I have the highest regard for him, and I think he does for me, also. Being in the company of David, Rich Valles, Dennis Rasmussen, and Joe O'Keefe there in Branson, gave me a comfortable feeling that I hadn't felt in a long time. It was like old home week for us.

Joseph "Doc" O'Keefe got out of the army after his time was up and went to work for the Electric Boat division of General Dynamics. I saw his name on an email posted on the 12th Cavalry website in 2006. He was looking for information about Pete Bentson, who is also from Connecticut. I got in touch with him and found out he was attending the 12th Cav reunion in Branson, MO. My wife and I immediately left for Branson. We had a great time together with him and his wife Pat. He recently had minor shoulder surgery. The pain blocker they put in his shoulder moved to his chest and collapsed his lung. He is now retired and living in Connecticut. We shared many memories and stories. I look forward to seeing him again. There is no finer guy anywhere.

Perry Benally survived his wounds and has lived on and off the reservation in New Mexico over the years. After

I found him, Charles Church and I talked with him by phone and found out that he never received any recognition for his heroic venture in December, 1967 at the Battle of Tam Quan. I got all the paperwork ready for submitting him for a Silver Star, 42 years after the fact. In August, 2010, I traveled to Gallup, New Mexico, to watch Senator Tom Udall present him with his richly deserved award. Evidently, the original paperwork was lost in our move up north to Quang Tri in early January of 1968.

Charley Waskey, our native Aluetian Indian, got out of the army and returned to Alaska. I'm sorry to report that he drank himself to death. He never got over the death of his friend, Rick Boeshart.

Spec. 5th Class "Doc" Michael Leroy is retired in Louisiana and disabled, with a heart condition. I hear from him quite frequently. I remember Doc as always throwing down his rifle when the bullets started flying. He never slacked in treating guys, no matter how many bullets were coming at us. After each firefight, we would always have to help him locate his rifle. He is another fine guy I've had the privilege of being associated with.

I was able to stop by Tuscaloosa, AL, in April 2009, to see *Billy Cabaniss* and his wife. Billy looked the same as he did in Vietnam, except for the gray hair and glasses. I've always had a deep affection for Billy. He was my radio operator on some of the more hairy "killer team" missions we ran around Quang Tri.

Staff Sgt. Delbert O. Jennings, my first squad leader, did receive the Medal of Honor from President Johnson. He stayed in the army and became the sergeant major of the 1st Cavalry Division at Ft. Hood, Texas. He passed away about five years ago in Honolulu. His son attends the 12th

Cavalry functions we have and brings his son to be with us. We have really enjoyed meeting him and getting to know him.

I answered an email in 2006, on the 12th Cav's website from a guy named *Dennis Horin*. Dennis claimed to have been with Charlie Company from May '67 to May '68. I didn't remember him, but I sent him an email anyway. About six months went by, and I got a call from Dennis. His voice and accent sounded strangely familiar. He is from New Jersey and told me he had contact with Walter Gutson, who is also from New Jersey and was wounded on May 31, 1967.

About five minutes into the conversation, I blurted out, "Are you the guy who fell off the bridge when we were on the cordon mission?" It was indeed Dennis. Dennis has his own public relations firm.

He told me, "Doug, I used to get in trouble for talking, so I decided to make a living at talking!"

In September 2007, I received a call from Tweek Van Dan, who spends so much of her time finding former members of Charlie Company. Tweek is the wife of Alan Van Dan, former secretary of the 12th Cavalry who wrote a column for the 1st Cav Association newsletter. She informed me she had found *Dennis "Torch" Rasmussen*. Dennis is an IT director for a community college in North Carolina. I contacted Dennis, and he came to the 12th Cavalry reunion in Branson, MO. We spent the better part of three days talking about all the good and bad times we had over the better part of a year in Vietnam. He was discharged from the army in 1968, and stayed out for over a year. He re-enlisted and returned to Vietnam and served with H Company, 75th Rangers, assigned to the 1st Cav.

He later re-joined the 1st of the 12th Cav and was with them until they returned to the States. He was an instructor in an NCO academy and was a drill sergeant at Fort Jackson, SC, until he got out in 1979. He had spent over eleven years of his life in the army.

In October 2007, I got an email from a veteran's service representative in California. She had just filled out forms for *Rich Valles*, my friend from California, who had just come into the VA for an appointment. I made contact with Rich and found out he had returned to the field one last time in May 1968 and was stranded when the helicopters could not return that night for him. They were hit with mortar fire and some shrapnel hit his cheek and destroyed the retina of his eye. He was medevaced and sent to The Presidio in San Francisco for treatment. He got out and returned to college to become a teacher and coach. He did that for thirty-six years and has recently retired. He raised four kids, two foster kids, and has a lot of grandchildren. I was excited to hear from him and know he was all right.

Some of our former officers in Charlie Company are worth mentioning here. Ralph Hagler went on to command the 75th Ranger, 2nd Battalion, in the '80s. He and his men made a combat jump from an altitude of five hundred feet into Grenada during the 1983 operation to oust the Cuban insurgents who were entrenched there. They didn't use reserve parachutes, as a reserve wouldn't have had time to deploy in case of malfunction, anyway. The last time I talked to Hagler, he was the Commander of the US Army Recruiting Command for the West Coast. The platoon leader for the 4th platoon was 1st Lt. Jim Schwebach, who went on to become a Special Forces captain and serve another tour in Vietnam. After the army, he joined the management team at EDS. When Ross Perot's employees were detained in Iran, Schwebach was on the assembled team to go in and get them out. I read about him later in Ken Follett's book, *On Wings of Eagles*. Both Schwebach and Hagler were good platoon leaders as was 1st Lt. Denny Lentsch, the platoon leader of the 1st platoon. We were blessed with great leaders in Charlie Company.

GLOSSARY

AO–Area of operations.

APC–Armored personnel carrier. A multi-wheeled, armored vehicle on tracks that could carry a squad of infantrymen. It had a door hatch for the driver, another for the TC (tank commander,) and a large hatch door for the rear of the carrier.

Army Commendation Medal with "V" Device–Lowest award for heroism or the fifth highest, depending on how you want to view it.

ARA–Aerial rocket artillery.

ARVN–Army of the Republic of Vietnam.

ASA–Army Security Agency.

AWOL–Absent without leave. Depending on the length of the absence from duty, the punishment could be either a fine or imprisonment.

Battalion–Army group made up of four companies comprised of about four hundred infantrymen total, plus their support groups.

Brigade–Army group made up of three battalions comprised of between 1,200 and 1,300 infantrymen total, plus their support groups.

Bronze Star with "V" Device–Fourth highest award for heroism in ground combat.

C-130–Medium range, four engine and propeller driven aircraft flown by the US Air Force. It can take off and land in short distances and hold sixty-four paratroopers with combat gear.

Click–Slang meaning a kilometer or one thousand meters on a map.

CO–Commanding officer.

CP–Command post, which consists of the commanding officer, the artillery forward observer, head medic, and the radiotelephone operators.

CQ–Charge of quarters. Extra duty assigned to non commissioned officers. The CQ was the ranking person in charge of the barracks from the early evening until early morning. He was responsible in case of emergency or if someone got sick during the night.

DEROS–Date estimated return (from) overseas (to) stateside.

DMZ–Demilitarized zone.

DSC–Distinguished Service Cross, the second highest award for heroism in combat.

Flanks–Two or three men, or a squad of men, who are to the right and left of a column on the march. Flanks are a necessity to keep from being ambushed.

HE–High explosive.

Ho Chi Minh–Leader of North Vietnam who lived in Hanoi.

Hollywood jump or exit–A jump without equipment, either from an airplane or an exit from a 34-foot jump tower.

KIA–Killed in action.

KP–Kitchen Police duty, which varies from washing pots and pans to peeling potatoes to mopping the mess hall.

LRP *or* **LRRP**–Long-Range Patrol or Long Range Reconnaissance Patrol.

LZ–Landing zone.

Medal of Honor–Highest award for combat, given for "service above and beyond the call of duty."

Mess hall–Where food is served to the soldiers. It can be a stationary building or a tent.

MOS–Military Occupational Specialty. Examples are infantry, artillery, judge advocate, engineer, etc.

M-16–Weapon issued to almost everyone in combat in Vietnam. It shoots a 5.56 mm round and can be fired on semi-automatic or full-automatic. The early M-16s in 1965 and 1966 fired too rapidly for the ejection system, so they jammed frequently.

M-60–Machine gun that shoots 7.62 mm rounds at a rate of approximately three hundred rounds per minute. Rounds can snap together into a belt.

M-79–Short-barreled gun that shoots either a 40 mm grenade or double aught buckshot round. The 40 mm grenade must travel at least eleven feet before it will arm itself and explode on impact.

NCO–Non-commissioned officer. Enlisted men who wear more than one stripe on their sleeves. In the army, that starts at corporal or sergeant.

NCOIC–Non commissioned officer in charge.

NVA–North Vietnamese Army.

Platoon Sergeant–The position is usually filled by a sergeant first class (E-7).

Profile–Term to describe soldiers who are recovering from injury and cannot be returned to duty until a designated time in the future.

PX–Post Exchange. Most Army bases and installations have a post exchange, which is like a department store.

RA–Regular army.

Silver Star–Third highest award for gallantry in action.

Soldier's Medal–Highest military award for life saving, not necessarily in combat.

SOP–Standard operating procedure.

RPG–Rocket propelled grenade.

RTO–Radiotelephone operator.

Track–Slang for armored personnel carrier.

TOC–Tactical operations center.

VC–Viet Cong.

WIA–Wounded in action.

XO–Executive officer.

PHOTOGRAPHS AND DOCUMENTS

This is the picture that my son took to college to show his ROTC friends that started all of the questions that led to the writing of this book.

Watching the artillery pound An Qui village the afternoon of May 31, 1967. That's me in the foreground.

Lt. Bob Radcliffe standing by the crater left from the detonation of the booby trap we almost stepped on in the Bong Son Plain in June 1967.

This picture was taken at a photography studio in Kontum, Vietnam, in July 1967, after a shower and new clothes. I had just made Specialist 4th Class.

The155 mm howitzer that was dropped on top of my foxhole by the flying crane that crashed and burned on July 3, 1967, on LZ Arbuckle. That's my foxhole at the bottom of the picture.

In the An Loa Valley in July 1967: Cliff Metz, Michael "Doc" Leroy, me, Tom Cusick, Rick Boeshart, and Charlie Waskey. Our pants legs are wet from crossing the An Loa River.

In September, 1967, I was at LZ Lowboy just before moving out to secure the bridges on Highway 1 before the national elections that month.

One of the machine gun crews in the 3rd platoon in the Bong Son Plain in the fall of 1967: Charley Waskey, assistant machine gunner; Rick Boeshart, machine gunner; and Larry Heath, ammo bearer.

The 1st squad of the 3rd platoon of Charlie Company in October 1967. Back row (L to R): Calvin Gouley, me, David Wilkowski, Phillip "Tyke" Hayes and Alvin Nibbelink. Kneeling (L to R): Buster Morgan and Luis Arroyo. All of us made it home.

I took this picture as I was about to leave for R&R at An Khe in early November 1967. The guys from 3rd platoon, Charlie Company, are getting their gear ready to go to Dak To. I recognize Luis Vincente (looking at the camera), Dennis Rasmussen (with the white hair), Rick Boeshart, David Wilkowski, Rich Valles, Aaron Foster, and Larry Heath.

I am standing in a Montagnard village in the mountains around Dak To in November 1967 with David Wilkowski, one of the M-79 men in my squad. He was the best M-79 gunner in our company.

In the Central Highlands of Vietnam, near Dak To, in 1967. Calvin Gouley (front) and David Wilkowski (rear) were in my squad. Rick Boeshart, carrying the machine gun, is in the middle.

1st Lt. Bob Radcliffe (right), West Point class of 1965, was the platoon leader of the 3rd platoon in mid 1967. He is the bravest man I've ever known, and I was proud to be associated with him.

Lt. Denny Lentsch, 1st platoon leader (later the XO), who took over command of Charlie Company on December 15–16, 1967, when Capt. Pete Bentson was medevaced out for a knee injury while we were engaged in the Battle of Tam Quan. Lentsch was a fine officer.

Spec. 4 Calvin Gouley with a prisoner we captured in the Bong Son Plain. Sitting on the porch are the company radio operators, Harold Bauer (left), Beuhler (center), and Bill Whitmore on the right.

Sgt. Cliff Metz (left) and me before an air assault at Quang Tri in February 1968.

Charlie Company troopers at the 12th Cavalry reunion in Branson, MO, September 2008: Larry Joe Bingham (May '68–May '69), Joe O'Keefe (May '67–May '68), me (May '67–May '68) and Dennis Rasmussen (May '67–May '68). We four were awarded twelve Purple Hearts.

Following are the orders for the awards and decorations I received. My last DD 214 (discharge) is also here. It doesn't list my parachutist badge, though my MOS ends with an "S," which means Special Forces Qualified. To be SF Qualified, you have to be a paratrooper. These documents have not been altered, except to remove my social security number on some of them. I did re-type, exactly, word for word, the General Order for my second Silver Star, since the original that I had was so badly discolored.

HEADQUARTERS
1ST CAVALRY DIVISION (AIRMOBILE)
APO San Francisco 96490

GENERAL ORDERS   23 September 1967
NUMBER   5778

AWARD OF THE BRONZE STAR MEDAL FOR HEROISM

1. TC 320. The following AWARD is announced.

WARDEN, DOUGLAS US54661773 PRIVATE FIRST CLASS E-3 United States Army
Company C, 1st Battalion (Airborne), 12th Cavalry

Awarded: Bronze Star Medal with "V" Device
Date action: 27 May 1967
Theater: Republic of Vietnam
Reason: For heroism in connection with military operations against a hostile
        force. Private First Class Warden distinguished himself by heroism
        in action on 27 May 1967, while serving as a radio-telephone operator
        with Company C, 1st Battalion (Airborne), 12th Cavalry during a sweep
        mission near An Do, Republic of Vietnam. When his unit came in con-
        tact with an enemy force, Private First Class Warden observed one of
        his comrades attempting to reach better cover after being pinned down
        by an enemy machine gun position. Disregarding his own safety, Pri-
        vate First Class Warden stood up between the enemy machine gunner and
        his comrade, engaged and killed the enemy machine gunner in a point-
        blank fire fight. Again engaged in a close combat assault, Private
        First Class Warden killed several more enemy soldiers and assisted in
        the capture of another. Private First Class Warden's display of per-
        sonal bravery and devotion to duty is in keeping with the highest tra-
        ditions of the military service, and reflects great credit upon him-
        self, his unit, and the United States Army.
Authority: By direction of the President, under the provisions of Executive
           Order 11046, 24 August 1962.

FOR THE COMMANDER:

OFFICIAL: GEORGE W. CASEY
                                     Colonel, GS
                                     Chief of Staff

Donald W Connelly
DONALD W. CONNELLY
LTC, AGC
Adjutant General

HEADQUARTERS
1ST CAVALRY DIVISION (AIRMOBILE)
APO San Francisco 96490

GENERAL ORDERS   3 September 1967
NUMBER   5076

AWARD OF THE SILVER STAR

1. TC 320. The following AWARD is announced.

WARDEN, DOUGLAS J. US54661773 PRIVATE FIRST CLASS E-3 United States Army
Company C, 1st Battalion (Airborne), 12th Cavalry

Awarded: Silver Star
Date action: 31 May 1967
Theater: Republic of Vietnam
Reason: For gallantry in action: Private First Class Warden distinguished
         himself by exceptionally valorous action on 31 May 1967, while
         serving as a radio-telephone operator with Company C, 1st Battalion
         (Airborne), 12th Cavalry during combat operations near the village
         of An Qui, Republic of Vietnam. When his company came into contact
         with a well-entrenched, numerically superior North Vietnamese Army
         force, one platoon was immediately pinned down and the others were
         engaged in an intense fire fight. Throughout the engagement, Private
         First Class Warden braved the intense enemy automatic weapons fire
         to remain with his platoon leader, despite the fact that the radio
         on his back made him a good target for the enemy gunners. At times,
         when his platoon was pinned down and surrounded on all sides, Pri-
         vate First Class Warden stood up and charged several bunkers with
         the platoon leader. Individually, he attacked several emplacements
         and destroyed them with hand grenades. Although new to combat, he
         continued to provide covering fire and excellent communications for
         his platoon leader, killing two or more North Vietnamese Army sol-
         diers from his exposed positions. Private First Class Warden's
         gallant action is in keeping with the highest traditions of the mili-
         tary service, and reflects great credit upon himself, his unit, and
         the United States Army.
Authority: By direction of the President, under the provisions of the Act
           of Congress, approved 9 July 1918, and USARV Message 16695,
           dated 1 July 1966.

FOR THE COMMANDER:

OFFICIAL: GEORGE W. CASEY
                                           Colonel, GS
                                           Chief of Staff

Donald W. Connelly
DONALD W. CONNELLY
ITC, AGC
Adjutant General

HEADQUARTERS
1ST CAVALRY DIVISION (AIRMOBILE)
APO San Francisco 96490

GENERAL ORDERS
NUMBER   5802

23 September 1967

AWARD OF THE SOLDIER'S MEDAL

1. TC 320. The following AWARD is announced.

WARDEN, DOUGLAS J. US54661773 SPECIALIST FOUR E-4 United States Army
Company C, 1st Battalion (Airborne), 12th Cavalry

Awarded: Soldier's Medal
Date action: 3 July 1967
Theater: Republic of Vietnam
Reason: For heroism not involving actual conflict with an armed enemy
force. Specialist Four Warden distinguished himself by heroism
on 3 July 1967, while serving as a radio-telephone operator with
Company C, 1st Battalion (Airborne), 12th Cavalry during a rescue
operation in the Republic of Vietnam. When a helicopter crashed
in an ammunition storage area, Specialist Warden moved forward to
the flaming wreckage and moved one of the injured crewman to a
safer area. Disregarding his own safety, Specialist Warden returned to the crash site and began moving boxes of ammunition away
from the wreck. He continued moving the ammunition until it was
all removed from the immediate area. His action saved several lives
and prevented a serious disaster. Specialist Warden's display of
personal bravery and devotion to duty is in keeping with the highest
traditions of the military service, and reflects great credit upon
himself, his unit, and the United States Army.
Authority: By direction of the President, under the provisions of the Act of
Congress, approved 2 July 1926.

FOR THE COMMANDER:

OFFICIAL:

Donald W. Connelly
DONALD W. CONNELLY
LTC, AGC
Adjutant General

GEORGE W. CASEY
Colonel, GS
Chief of Staff

DEPARTMENT OF THE ARMY
HEADQUARTERS, 1ST AIR CAVALRY
APO San Francisco 96490

GENERAL ORDERS   13 July 1968
NUMBER 8110

AWARD OF THE SILVER STAR w/ 1st Oak Leaf Cluster

    1. TC 320. The following AWARD is announced.

WARDEN, DOUGLAS J. US54661773 STAFF SERGEANT E-6 United
States Army Company C, 1st Battalion (Airborne), 12th Cavalry

Awarded: Silver Star
Date action: 15 December 1967
Theater: Republic of Vietnam
Reason: For gallantry in action while engaged in military operations involv-
    ing conflict with an armed hostile force in the Republic of Vietnam.
    Staff Sergeant Warden distinguished himself by exceptionally valorous
    action on 15 December 1967 while serving as a squad leader with Company C, 1st
    Battalion (Airborne), 12th Cavalry during a combat operation near Bong Son Plains,
    Republic of Vietnam. When his unit came under heavy enemy fire, Staff Sergeant
    Warden deployed his men in such a manner as to avoid being pinned down. He then
    led an assault on an anti-tank position and eliminated it. Disregarding his own
    safety, Staff Sergeant Warden exposed himself to the hostile fire as he rescued a
    mortally wounded soldier. His gallant action is in keeping with the highest traditions of
    the military of the military service, and reflects great credit upon himself, his unit, and
    the United States Army.

Authority: By direction of the President, under the provisions of the Act of
    Congress, approved 9 July 1918.

    FOR THE COMMANDER:

OFFICIAL   CONRAD L. STANSBERRY
                                         Colonel, GS
                                         Chief of Staff

LESTER J. EVANS
LTC, AGC
Adjutant General

DISTRIBUTION   **SPECIAL DISTRIBUTION**
2 – AG-ASD   1 –AGPERSCEN, ATTN: WGPE-F
10 – AVDAAG-AD   Ft. Benjamin Harrison, Ind 46216
2 – AVDAAG – R
1 – G1
2 – USARV, ATTN: AVAGP-D

THIS IS AN IMPORTANT RECORD
SAFEGUARD IT.

1. LAST NAME–FIRST NAME–MIDDLE NAME	2. SERVICE NUMBER	3. SOCIAL SECURITY NUMBER
WARDEN DOUGLAS JASON	RA 54 661 773	

PERSONAL DATA

4. DEPARTMENT, COMPONENT AND BRANCH OR CLASS	5a. GRADE, RATE OR RANK	5b. PAY GRADE	6. DATE OF RANK
ARMY RA – UNASGD	SSG	E-6	Jun 69

7. U.S. CITIZEN ☒ YES ☐ NO   8. PLACE OF BIRTH — Prague Oklahoma   9. DATE OF BIRTH

12a. SELECTIVE SERVICE NUMBER				b. SELECTIVE SERVICE LOCAL BOARD NUMBER, CITY, COUNTY, STATE AND ZIP CODE	DATE INDUCTED
34	65	47	119	Local Board No 65 Shawnee (Pottawatomie) Oklahoma 74801	NA

SELECTIVE SERVICE DATA

11a. TYPE OF TRANSFER OR DISCHARGE	8. STATION OR INSTALLATION AT WHICH EFFECTED
Retired	Brooke Army Medical Center Ft Sam Houston Texas

c. REASON AND AUTHORITY	EFFECTIVE DATE	2 Mar 73

d. LAST DUTY ASSIGNMENT AND MAJOR COMMAND	13a. CHARACTER OF SERVICE	b. TYPE OF CERTIFICATE ISSUED
400th USASASOD (Abn) Ryukyu Islands	HONORABLE	DD Form 363A

TRANSFER OR DISCHARGE

14. DISTRICT, AREA COMMAND OR CORPS TO WHICH RESERVIST TRANSFERRED — NA

15. TERMINAL DATE OF RESERVE/MILITIA OBLIGATION	17. CURRENT ACTIVE SERVICE OTHER THAN BY INDUCTION	16. TERM OF SERVICE	DATE OF ENTRY
NA	a. SOURCE OF ENTRY: ☐ ENLISTED (First Enlistment) ☐ ENLISTED (Prior Service) ☒ REENLISTED ☐ OTHER	4	9 Jul 71

18. PRIOR REGULAR ENLISTMENTS	19. GRADE, RATE OR RANK AT TIME OF ENTRY INTO CURRENT ACTIVE SVC	20. PLACE OF ENTRY INTO CURRENT ACTIVE SERVICE (City and State)
NA	SSG (E-6)	USASASFS Sobe APO SF 96331

SERVICE DATA

21. HOME OF RECORD AT TIME OF ENTRY INTO ACTIVE SERVICE	22.	STATEMENT OF SERVICE	YEARS	MONTHS	DAYS
Route 1 Prague (Lincoln) Oklahoma 74864		(1) NET SERVICE THIS PERIOD	1	7	24
	CREDITABLE FOR BASIC PAY PURPOSES	(2) OTHER SERVICE	5	0	11
23a. SPECIALTY NUMBER & TITLE		(3) TOTAL (Line (1) plus Line (2))	6	8	5
98C4S Traffic	b. TOTAL ACTIVE SERVICE		5	2	27
Analyst (Aug72)	NA	c. FOREIGN AND OR SEA SERVICE RYI	1	11	5

24. DECORATIONS, MEDALS, BADGES, COMMENDATIONS, CITATIONS AND CAMPAIGN RIBBONS AWARDED OR AUTHORIZED

Silver Star with First Oak Leaf Cluster – Purple Heart with Second Oak Leaf Cluster – Army Commendation Medal – Combat Infantryman Badge – Air Medal – Soldier's Medal – Bronze Star with "V" Device – National Defense Service Medal – Good Conduct Medal

25. EDUCATION AND TRAINING COMPLETED

None

26a. NON-PAY PERIODS TIME LOST (Preceding Two Years)	b. DAYS ACCRUED LEAVE PAID	27a. INSURANCE IN FORCE (USGLI or NSLI)	b. AMOUNT OF ALLOTMENT	c. MONTH ALLOTMENT DISCONTINUED
None	None	☐ YES ☒ NO	NA	NA

VA AND SVC. SEPARATION DATA

28. VA CLAIM NUMBER	29. SERVICEMEN'S GROUP LIFE INSURANCE COVERAGE
C- 24 121 094	☒ $15,000 ☐ $10,000 ☐ $5,000 ☐ NONE

30. REMARKS

13 Years Schooling   Blood Group – "O+"

REMARKS

31. PERMANENT ADDRESS FOR MAILING PURPOSES AFTER TRANSFER OR DISCHARGE	32. SIGNATURE OF PERSON BEING TRANSFERRED OR DISCHARGED
31 Bonnie Sue Box 85 Meeker (Lincoln) Oklahoma 74855	
33. TYPED NAME, GRADE AND TITLE OF AUTHORIZING OFFICER	34. SIGNATURE OF OFFICER AUTHORIZED TO SIGN
ALBERT J SIERRA JR CPT MSC ASST ADJUTANT	

AUTHENTICATION

DD FORM 1 JUL 70 214   PREVIOUS EDITION OF THIS FORM TO BE USED.   ARMED FORCES OF THE UNITED STATES REPORT OF TRANSFER OR DISCHARGE   2

DEPARTMENT OF THE ARMY
OFFICE OF THE ADJUTANT GENERAL
WASHINGTON, D.C. 20314

DAAG-PSS-R   23 Feb 73

LETTER ORDERS NUMBER D 2-584

SUBJECT: Enlisted Disability Retirement

SSG DOUGLAS J. WARDEN
        98C4S
Brooke General Hospital
Fort Sam Houston, TX 78234

TC 375. The above named individual having been determined to be **PERMANENTLY**
unfit for duty by reason of physical disability, is relieved from **assignment**
and duty and placed on the RETIRED LIST as indicated.

ADMINISTRATIVE ACCOUNTING DATA
Auth (Ret): 10 USC 1201
Place ret: Meeker, OK
SPN: 271
PCS MDC: 7BE3
Eff date (REFRAD): 2 Mar 73

FOR THE INDIVIDUAL
Date placed on retired list: 3 Mar 73
Retired grade: SSG
Percentage of disability: 30%
Special Instructions (APPENDIX B, AR 310-10): 83

BY ORDER OF THE SECRETARY OF THE ARMY:

P.M. Mitchell

Adjutant General